What Makes You Tic?

What Makes You Tic?

My Journey From Tourette's To Tolerance

Marc Elliot

Let Live Publishing
New York

Let Live Publishing
New York, NY

ISBN: 978-0-615-55675-8

Printed by BookMasters Inc., of Mansfield, Ohio.

Cover Illustration by Andrea Levy

To Dr. Jesse Ternberg –
I will always be your tough bird!

Acknowledgments

It's taken an army of people to get me here today, alive and with a book to show for it. I would like to thank every single one of them. None of us is truly independent, me less than most.

To the stranger on the street who told another stranger I had Tourette's to make my day a little easier, thank you.

To everyone in the medical profession who helped cure me and heal me, thank you.

To my teachers, counselors, administrators and coaches who taught me, guided me, and enriched my life, thank you.

To all of my friends who offered me companionship, solace and fun, thank you.

To all the individuals who have provided me insight, advice, coaching and just plain hard work to help me spread my message of tolerance, thank you.

To John Bowe, who helped me bring my story to life in a way I could have never imagined possible, thank you.

To my younger brother, Justin, who has ultimately become one of my greatest teachers in life, thank you.

To my older brother, Brian, who is the closest thing to an idol I have ever known, thank you.

To my parents who spoiled me with unconditional love and repeatedly managed the impossible throughout my life, thank you.

Finally, to the reader, thank you for reading this book. I hope you find it a wonderful experience.

Many of the names of people who appear in this book have been changed to protect their privacy.

Introduction

Once upon a time, when I was in high school, my AP U.S. History teacher was writing something on the board. It wasn't a very exciting moment in class – or, for that matter, in U.S. history. In fact, it was kind of boring. So I spoke up about it. Right? Honesty is always the best policy. I said, in a fairly loud voice, "Boring!" Everyone turned to look at me, and I said it again, even more loudly. "Boring!!" My teacher turned around, very slowly. He looked at me, knowing who I was, and said, "Yeah, yeah."

That probably would have been enough for most students, but I wasn't done yet. I hadn't made it a full Marc Elliot moment. So then I said, still louder, "F..k you!!"

Does blurting out "Boring!" in the middle of some boring class sound like a dream come true for you? I have to admit that sometimes it was. I was a kid who could get away with such outbursts. They were just considered typical behavior for me at that age. But it wasn't because I was so rebellious or cool. It was because of a problem I have called Tourette syndrome.

Tourette syndrome causes me to jerk and bite and shake my head and sniff and blink and do all kinds of weird stuff, including acting disruptively and disrespectfully in class.

These things I do are involuntary impulses called "tics." I can't help them any more than you can help blinking. I've had these tics since I was six, at a rate of about three per minute. They're very distracting. Each one last about three seconds and interrupts whatever I'm doing. I'm 26 now, so if you add them up over the course of my entire life, I've probably ticced about 21 million times. That comes out to about 1,497,965 minutes, or 24,966 hours, of my life spent jiggling, jerking, and doing things that make people think I'm a freak.

But it gets worse. Ten percent of people with Tourette's have something called coprolalia, which means they involuntarily use inappropriate language. I'm one of the 10 percent. I use horrible language, constantly, right in front of people and in the most embarrassing, offensive, humiliating way, both for me and for the people I offend.

That started when I was in 10th grade. And then it got worse. And worse. Adjusting for the good and bad years, I've probably said the word "f..k" or "f.....r," about 6,000 times. I've probably said "p...y" or "c..t," about 3,000 times. "Fa..ot" and "You're gay" have always been popular — I bet I've said those about 4,500 times each. Then there's probably the worst single word in the English language: "n....r." I bet I've said that about 7,000 times.

Imagine being me for a second: walking into a room with someone who's overweight and saying, "Fat! You're fat!!" or "I want to f..k you!" Or, as I said many, many times and very loudly at a bus station, far from home, where dozens and dozens of black people were waiting, "N....r! N....r!!"

Do you think that sounds like a stressful way to go through life? Let's just say my life hasn't always been easy.

But it gets more complicated. Because, in addition to my Tourette's, I have *another* rare condition, an intestinal disease called Hirschsprung's. To cut to the chase, it makes me have the loudest poops in the world. They last about 10 minutes each and happen five to eight times a day, anywhere I happen to be – at home, in restaurants, in schools and in other public places.

Because of these two enormous medical challenges, I have had a very different life from most people. I have never had the luxury of keeping secrets or hiding my problems. In my private life and even in public, people figure out very quickly: This guy has problems. There have been times when this has made my life very painful. Yet, despite my problems, I've managed to live a happy life. I have friends. I travel. I have girlfriends (sometimes). Somehow, I'm not a miserable wretch. I'm successful. I like my life.

Instead of ruining my life, my problems have, more than anything, enabled me to tell a very funny story (yes, it's funny sometimes to be the guy who says "You suck! I'm bored!!!" to his teachers). And to talk about something more interesting, which is *how* I manage to deal with my problems.

I will tell you that, despite the naughty words and the emphasis in this book on funny poop noises, this is a story of triumph over adversity like you've never heard before. This book tells how I have learned to embrace my life and not die of embarrassment every morning, afternoon, and night.

One of my goals in writing this book is simply to educate people about Tourette syndrome. There are an estimated 200,000 Americans afflicted with Tourette's. If each of these people comes from a family of four, then that makes close to a million people in the United States whose lives have been seriously affected by Tourette's. For these individuals alone, it's important to help pave the way to greater societal understanding.

But my story isn't just about Tourette's. Or about pooping disorders. It's about tolerance. How do we learn to tolerate our problems? How do we learn to tolerate other people's problems?

My story is about living a life with two incredibly unique challenges. They have allowed me to gain a perspective on life that few other people experience. This perspective of seeing how people treat someone so different than everyone else has given me the opportunity to learn some fundamental lessons about tolerance.

By sharing experiences of my life – the challenges I have faced and the many people I have met along my journey – I illustrate how tolerance can be a source of strength. My hope is that, after you finish reading this book, you can think about tolerance and differences among people in a way you have never before.

When I tell the details of how ridiculously embarrassing my problems can be, people laugh. Why? Because my problems have been so outlandish and dramatic that they're funny. What happens next is that people tend to accept me. The moment they realize it's OK to laugh at me (and with me because I'm laughing, too), they realize that having problems is not the end of the world. A person can be a perfectly worthwhile human being, even if they're not perfect. The next thing that happens is people see that it is beneficial to TALK about problems instead of hiding them. And finally, people begin to think about their own lives: Why do I worry so much about other people's problems? Why do I even worry so much about my own problems?

As a public speaker, I meet hundreds of people every week — people with difficult problems or with simply things they don't like about themselves. They share their stories with me: They're shy, gay, pregnant, addicted to drugs, depressed, victims of racism, racist themselves, victims of bad parents, victims of older siblings, too smart, too rich, too fat, too this, too that. What I've learned is that it's not just me who has embarrassing problems: It's most of us. So this story goes way beyond Tourette's and having no intestines.

It doesn't matter what our problems are. What's important is how we deal with them. How do we learn to accept ourselves and tolerate other people as they are? How do we learn to spend less time being anxious about all the things we don't like about other people or about ourselves?

I don't have all the answers. And I won't pretend that my story will make all the people of the world want to run out into a big meadow somewhere in their bare feet, join hands and dance around with daisies in their hair. But after meeting thousands of people, young

and old, all over the country in the past couple of years, I have definitely learned there are ways to deal with problems that can help us
all become much happier.

I hope that my journey from constant embarrassment to freedom
(not 100% freedom, but what I call "most-of-the-time-freedom") will
help people find ways to relax and spend less time judging themselves and others. In my experience, learning to be a bit more tolerant
has made all the difference in the world.

I've never been sure if my earliest memory was a dream or if it really happened. Either way, this is how I remember the beginning of my life: I see a picture of a little boy in shorts and a short-sleeved shirt sitting in a doctor's office. The room is green, and I'm sitting on one of those examination tables covered with that hygienic wax paper. The paper crinkles beneath my legs.

There is a doctor there, putting a mask on me, trying to get me to lie down and sleep. I'm not fighting him, but I'm not asleep yet. I'm not terrified, exactly, but it's uncomfortable. The room smells distinctly of something noxious. Disinfectant, maybe. To this day, I can recall the smell.

None of this is important. Except that if you were to ask kids what their earliest memory is, most would say nothing about a hospital or a doctor's office.

That wasn't the case with me.

My family was pretty traditional in many ways. Most ways, in fact.

My dad grew up in Pueblo, Colorado. He had a pretty tumultuous childhood. His mother and sister both had serious health issues, and his childhood was characterized by a lot of yelling. His dad worked in a steel factory. On the outside, his life was as vanilla as you could imagine. He had the same lunch – a ham sandwich – every day for 30 years in a row.

My mom grew up in the suburbs of Detroit. She had an older brother and a younger sister. Her mom stayed at home; her dad worked as a pharmacist. Hers was a pretty intense childhood as well. Very vanilla on the outside, but darker on the inside. Again, lots of yelling.

They met in Boulder, at the University of Colorado. My mom double-majored in education and communications, and my dad studied engineering. They dated, fell in love instantly and got married right after they graduated.

My dad's first job was in Cape Girardeau, Missouri, about two hours south of St. Louis. Even the people who live there call it "the boonies."

My parents felt like fish out of water – two Jews living in the middle of nowhere. At one point, someone asked my mom where her horns were. The person had never met a Jew before, and I guess they had some funny ideas about what to expect. My mom started working as a teacher in a school that had corporal punishment (spanking, ruler-smacking and so on) and segregated classrooms. I don't think my parents were very happy there. When my dad got offered a job in St. Louis in the jewelry business, he jumped at the opportunity.

Four years after they got married, my brother Brian was born. Even before his arrival, my parents had committed themselves to being there for their kids more than their parents had been. They wanted stability and money, so they worked hard. Their bookshelves were lined with books about how to be good parents.

Both my mom and my dad were looking to reinvent themselves, to create a life for themselves that their parents hadn't given them. Once they got to St. Louis, they set out to be very social and take part in the community. And that's what they did. They had tons of friends. They became active in their temple. They got involved with the school system.

My mom worked taking phone reservations for Trans World Airlines (TWA), a once-huge airline that no longer exists. She did that for 14 years even though she hated the job. My dad worked for a few years in the jewelry business. He didn't like it much and didn't make enough money. One day my father met a man who looked well-off and drove a nice car. My dad asked him what he did for a living, and the guy said he was a stockbroker. My dad's been a stockbroker ever since.

By the time I came along in 1985, my parents lived in a two-story house in a place called Chesterfield. Our house sat at the bottom of a hill, on a cul-de-sac on Tullytown Lane. There were three other houses, and all our back yards adjoined, so we kids had this big huge area to play in.

Chesterfield was mainly a white community, with a small number of minorities. The school system was desegregated, which meant kids from the city of St. Louis were bused to our school. Most of the kids were black. The neighborhood I grew up in was probably more diverse than the rest of the town. We were friends with most of our neighbors. Behind our house were the Waxes (Wendy, Sandy, Steve and Jeff). To the left of us were the Daultanays (Rabab and Aamir). They were from Pakistan. Whenever their mom wanted them to come home, she'd step out the front door and clap her hands. The smell of curry would come wafting out the door. The moment she clapped, Rabab and Aamir went running like crazy for the door. They would never have dreamt of dawdling or ignoring their mother for a second. The woman scared me to death. Our other neighbors were Iranian Jews. And then there were the Sarantos, who were Greek. So, in the middle of this predominantly white American suburb, my school and my neighborhood were a pretty mixed bunch. Despite the diversity of backgrounds, my hometown was the epitome of American suburbia.

We had the Chesterfield Mall. There was the Brunswick bowling alley. There was the AMC 12, which had a dozen movie theaters. There were the standard strip malls and restaurants like Noble Roman's, where you could watch them make your pizza through the window. There was Pasta House and fancier places like Spiro's, a Greek restaurant with candles on the tables. And then there was the Chinese place, Hunan Empress, where all the Jews like us would go on Christmas.

I was born on August 12, 1985, a Monday. At first I seemed perfectly healthy. I had a fuzzy head of hair, and I was bright-eyed and active. But after a while, the doctors noticed I wasn't pooping. Tuesday came, and I still wasn't pooping. Wednesday, same thing. Finally, they wheeled over the portable X-ray machine and x-rayed my digestive system to see if something might be wrong. Bad news. Doctors couldn't tell if it was cystic fibrosis or something called a meconium plug or what it was. But something was very wrong with my intestines. Suddenly, everything went into high speed. Thursday morning, they rolled me on my little gurney from the regular part of the hospital, through the elevators and across the walkway to the Children's Hospital next door. They immediately started to prep me for surgery.

The head of surgery explained the situation to my parents, but everything was such a blur and seemed so scary that it went over their heads. All they heard was the single line, repeated several times in grave tones: "You have a very sick baby." They were in shock. Three days earlier, they'd had a perfectly healthy baby. All of a sudden, I was in intensive care, and my life was at risk.

My surgeon's name was Dr. Jesse Ternberg. She wasn't even supposed to be on call that night, but, in the end, she would save my life – many times over. The surgery revealed that I had a rare form of something called Hirschsprung's disease. Among other things, it meant that I had only four feet of working intestines, compared to about 7 or 8 feet for a normal infant. I couldn't have digested food even if I could have eaten it.

Hirschsprung's today isn't quite as life-threatening, but, even as recently as 1985, doctors didn't have very good tools for dealing with advanced cases. The protocol at the hospital at that time was that anyone born with less than 5 feet of working intestines shouldn't be operated on. Dr. T knew that. And she knew that if anyone else knew that, I would, for all intents and purposes, be left to die.

So for the first three months of my life, she didn't exactly go out of her way to mention this to anyone. If any of the doctors from the other departments had known, they couldn't have performed all the many surgeries they would eventually complete. It would have been forbidden. This was not because they were mean or crazy or stingy. It's just that kids with my particular set of problems didn't tend to live very long. Hospitals had simply learned from experience that pouring resources into a lost cause often bankrupts families financially and emotionally, ruining the lives of all those related to the sick kid. It wasn't an easy choice for anyone.

There was a moment when Dr. T grilled my mom and dad about the family. My parents felt that she was trying to get a sense of who they were in order to decide whether our family could handle the ride we were in for.

What were my parents like as a couple? How suited to being parents were they? How much money did they have? Did they have a strong network of family and friends who could watch our backs and help us if we were about to enter years of stressful existence? Luckily, my mom and dad had built a strong family core with adequate financial means. Giving me a chance at life was a huge risk for everyone – my family and the doctor – financially, emotionally and professionally. Dr. T decided to take the risk.

On her orders, this whole big team of surgeons, nurses, aides, everyone was persuaded to go along with a complicated set of surgeries. First, they performed an ileostomy, which means they closed off my anus, took my ileum (part of the small intestine), poked it through my stomach and connected it to a colostomy bag. For the next two and a half years, my poop ended up in a bag outside my belly. (I know: hot!)

Later, Dr. T performed extremely experimental surgeries to reconnect parts of my intestines to each other to create a special pouch so that I could still get nutrients. Otherwise, I would have been on a feeding tube my whole life.

For my first six months, I was on a type of treatment called TPN, or Total Parenteral Nutrition, which is basically just a feeding tube with nutrients. Until around 1985, this had been considered very experimental treatment as well. There was little data to show that kids could thrive or even survive on it for long. The treatment had an unfortunate tendency to destroy all other organs. Dr. T was taking an enormous risk. The treatment had only recently been deemed worthy, although still risky. I probably wouldn't have made it, and a lot of effort and money would have gone down the drain.

During the time I was on TPN, the nutrients I needed to survive came from machines. Dr. T knew that could have long-term consequences. I might never learn how to eat or even speak properly. So Dr. T encouraged my mom to try to breastfeed me as soon as I got out of intensive care and then had my parents feed me a special formula they called "liquid platinum." The feedings kept me from developing oral hypersensitivity, an all-too-frequent problem among kids like me.

For weeks, then months, all those feedings happened in the hospital. I never left. I never went home.

My hospital room was right across from the nursing station. My parents decorated it with all kinds of colorful things so it wouldn't look so institutional. They draped a big huge kite with a 30-foot-long tail across the ceiling and hung mobiles with pictures of themselves so that I could feel like they were close. They brought in a musical clown with lights. But no matter what they did to decorate my room, I was in a hospital, not a home.

What follows comes from my parents of course: I was too young to remember. My ileostomy bag was painful. It wouldn't stay on well because a little bit of stool was always leaking out. Stool is acidic so it would eat away at the seal, and the bag would slip around, creating rashes and irritation on my baby skin. Nurses had to change the bag two or three times a day. One time, it broke all over me. I was in constant discomfort. My grandpa was so freaked out by seeing me with the ileostomy bag and all these tubes coming out everywhere, he almost didn't want to come visit me.

Dr. T was always very cautious about getting my parents' hopes up. She never promised them things like, "Oh, he'll be home in a month." No one ever knew what was going to happen or when I was going to come home or if I was going to come home.

My father felt particularly helpless seeing me in my little hospital bed, hooked up to machines for so long. I was missing out on the physical bonding that happens between kids and their parents. He remembered the many times that my brother Brian had been naked with my father and mother as a baby, cuddled up beside them, receiving the physical warmth that is so important to a kid's well-being. In fact, many emerging medical studies show that kids' emotional well-being in adulthood is determined by how much time they are held by their parents when they're young. My father worried that I was missing out on that. It seemed so cold, so alien, for a kid not to be able to touch his parents. One day, when I was two months old, he snuck me out of my room and walked over to the waiting room, where there was a couch. He lay down, opened his shirt, opened my nightie, and laid me down on his chest. I went to sleep. Finally, there I was, sleeping next my dad, touching, skin-to-skin.

In January, when I was five months old, Dr. T told my parents they could take me home. They both say it was the happiest day of their lives. They went crazy. They drove like maniacs to the hospital, grabbed all my stuff and piled it into the car. I can only imagine how they felt as they were driving home with me in the car. As my dad told me later, they had never really known whether I was going to make it home to the crib they'd bought for me.

Before I was even born, they had gone to great lengths preparing my room. They'd painted it yellow. They'd gotten this hip, modern crib painted with all different colors and some light maple wood furniture, a little rocking chair and a dresser with different-colored knobs. There was a little stool with the letters "M-A-R-C" painted on it. Everything looked perfect. Finally, I was home! Maybe everything would settle down, and life as a family could begin all over again. Wrong. A week after I went home from the hospital, I got something called rotavirus that caused horrible diarrhea. I had to go back to the hospital. I almost died—again. I stayed there for more than a month.

By the time I was four years old, I'd had seven surgeries. For each surgery, my parents would hand me off to the nurses. The nurses would disappear with me through the surgery doors, and my parents would never know if I was going to make it back or not. It was completely traumatic for them. It wasn't until the seventh, and final, surgery that I began to experience anything like a normal life.

I was still being rushed back and forth to the hospital. Day-to-day life was filled with a high degree of panic. But in retrospect, it's clear that we'd already passed the high-water mark of risk. From that point on, there would still be many problems to face, but they would be of a less life-and-death nature.

I had had so many surgeries and so much internal exposure to latex from doctors' gloves that I became insanely allergic to latex. It wouldn't be such a big deal except that no one knew it for several years. Once, I was in the basement with some friends, playing doctor. I found some latex gloves and put them on. Suddenly, I broke out in hives all over my face. Another time, I went to a birthday party where there was a rabbit. I had some kind of reaction and started to swell up. Everyone freaked out, thinking that I might be allergic to rabbits. Probably it was a reaction to the balloon I had played with.

In both cases, my parents gave me a Benadryl, and everything was fine. Later, after testing, doctors discovered the latex allergy. They gave me something called an EpiPen to carry around at all times. An EpiPen is a big long needle hidden inside something that looks like a magic marker. If you go into anaphylactic shock from a bad allergic reaction, you jab the EpiPen into your thigh. The needle pops out of the plastic casing and gives you a big shot of adrenaline.

My parents had been financially secure before I came along, but you can imagine how much all of the medical procedures cost. My father was self-employed, so we had only my mom's health insurance – and a lot of stuff wasn't covered by her plan. TWA held a fundraiser for me. I think my parents felt humiliated to have to rely on outside help, but it made a huge difference.

It's an understatement to say that my recovery and survival were miraculous. I was on the news. They put my picture on posters in the hospital. I was known as the "miracle baby."

Dr. T became and remained very close to our family. On the one hand, she tried to remain slightly impersonal. After all, it's not very professional – or even helpful, in some ways – for doctors to get too emotionally involved with their patients. On the other hand, imagine being a doctor. This little baby comes into your life. The baby's life is up in the air. You operate on him seven times, you hold him in your hands, you see him several days a week for four years. You save his life. After all you've been through together, you're going to have some kind of bond with the kid. And Dr. T did. We called her my "other mother."

Dr. T always called me her "tough bird." She told me that her favorite animal was the penguin. She admired it because it can survive the harsh winter of Antarctica. So for my whole life, my favorite animal has also been the penguin. I used to have dozens of stuffed penguins in my room. I guess it was my way of having a relationship with Dr. T and reflected the huge influence she had had on my life.

It was a very, very powerful thing to be aware from such a young age that this person, this lady, this doctor, had held the keys to my life and had used them in such a way that allowed me to be here, breathing. She had watched me fight through every challenge. It was like a partnership, in a weird way. She gave me the tools to live, and I grabbed onto them, even before I could speak. And together, we pulled me back into life.

Even though I had a lot of ongoing health issues, my energy normalized. It took me very little time to turn into a normal boy – in most ways. I became confident, assertive and more or less charismatic, which was great, because by all rights, I could have ended up being a feeble, shell-shocked kid. My emotional confidence level was just fine, and I showed no signs of being traumatized.

I got to run and play outside with our neighbors. Summer or winter, our motley little cul-de-sac gang never stopped playing. Our back yards provided the ultimate soccer field. The street in front was perfect for foursquare and street hockey. In and out of the houses and bushes, across the lawns and around the mailboxes, we played tag.

By first grade, I'd become the fastest runner in the class. By the time I was six, seven years old, you would never know there had ever been anything wrong with me. Only if you saw me without a shirt would you notice the scars stretching across my abdomen.

When medical crises came about, they came about in a slightly less stressful context. I still faced lots of problems, but fewer emergencies. Life went up, and then it went down again. Things were better, but never easy.

Every time I got a normal flu or diarrhea or food poisoning, I ran the risk of getting dehydrated. My intestinal problems had left me with a diminished ability to absorb water, so dehydration was always a danger. Hundreds of times my mom would look across from me at the dinner table and notice that I had little bags developing under my eyes. She'd say, "You look dehydrated." And this was not even when I was sick. I would just sort of look lethargic. Most of the time, we could deal with it at home by forcing me to rehydrate. Many times, though, we would have to rush to the hospital to replenish my fluids. I probably went back to Children's Hospital a dozen or more times to get an emergency rehydration. They would hook me up to an IV and feed me bags of saline solution.

The second they started pumping the fluid into me, my energy would start coming back. I would sit there for three hours, while two or three bags of solution would get injected into my body. I wouldn't have even been aware that I was losing all my energy, and then it would hit me: "Boom. I'm alive again." It was like recharging an appliance.

Another recurring issue was the routine vitamin B-12 shots. B-12, unlike many nutrients, is absorbed in the last part of the small intestine, which is called the ileum. I didn't have an ileum, so I couldn't absorb it. Every week or two, my mom and I would pile into the Chrysler minivan and drive downtown to get an injection. (I still need them once a month, but I administer them myself.)

I was so accustomed to hospitals, needles and IVs and the emergency room that they all seemed kind of cool and fun. I knew the ER nurse by her first name, Robin. I remember the ER, too, as well as I remember my own house: It was a very long rectangular room, and on the north and south walls, there were windows. By the north wall, there were games for kids. One of them was this rickety setup with all these metal wires. You would put a ball somewhere in the whole contraption, and it would set in motion all of these other reactions. Sort of like the game Mouse Trap.

We would wait there. I would play. They would call my name. And then we'd walk across the hallway, enter a sort of dark, mustard-yellow cubicle, and there would be Robin, waiting for me by the examination table. I would jump up on it, she'd give me my shot, and then my mom would take me to the first-floor gift shop and buy me a few Tootsie Rolls. I remember this even more vividly than I remember any of my birthdays.

Every time I went to the hospital, they would give me a hospital bracelet with my name and date of birth. To me, those bracelets were like little badges of honor because they said, "Look, I just came back from the hospital!! Look at me!" I would come home, tug my bracelet off and save it in my drawer, along with dozens of others. I felt like superman. No one had more hospital bracelets than me!

After a while, it became less fun and less cool to go to the hospital. I was beginning to know my body. One time, I started getting dehydrated, and I really didn't want to have to go down to Children's, so I started slamming Gatorade – red Gatorade. I drank six bottles in a row. I kept slamming them down and then, immediately, throwing them back up. I just couldn't hold the fluids down. But the attempt to avoid yet another trip to the hospital was a sign that I was beginning to grow up, in my own strange way.

One outcome of my Hirschsprung's was that my bowel movements were liquid. Yes, liquid – 100 percent of the time. Because I had no large intestine, and only four feet of small intestine, to absorb them, liquids just passed through me. In other words, I had diarrhea every single time. Voilà: liquid poops.

I was completely incontinent while sleeping, which means that, like a baby, I had no control over my bowels. They just did whatever they wanted to. I slept in diapers until fourth grade. Every night, my parents would put pads on my bed. Every morning, I would wake up covered in my own poop. My parents would walk into my room, pick up my legs, wipe me clean, take off the diaper, throw it away and put new pads on the bed. That was how we began every day.

Friends would occasionally ask me to come to their house for a sleepover. For many years, of course, I didn't want anyone to know about all my poop issues. What was I supposed to say? Certainly, none of the other kids was wearing diapers anymore. How was I going to get through a night at anyone's house but my own?

My mother came up with an ingenious solution. She tucked a diaper into my sleeping bag. I'd go to the sleepover. And at night, when my friends and I went to bed, I'd change into my diaper. Then, in the morning, I'd wait in my sleeping bag until everyone left the room, slide the diaper off, put it back in the bottom of the sleeping bag, then run to the front door and put it outside for my mom to swing by and grab it. Problem solved. No one ever knew.

When I was 10 years old, I decided that I really wanted to go to this Jewish sleep-away camp. This meant that I would need to learn how to get by without my diapers. I was a deep sleeper, and I never got into the habit of waking up to go to the bathroom. My mom found a doctor in Kansas who had invented a machine that cured people of bed-wetting. It was this crazy-looking contraption with an electric pad that you slept on top of. It looked like a miniature fire truck or something, with all these strobe lights and a siren. The pad was hooked up to all of these things, and, if the sensors inside detected any liquid, "Ding! Ding! Ding! Ding!" All these strobes and sirens went off! You could hear it throughout the entire house.

It was meant to be so loud and jarring that it woke you up, and it was intended for bed-wetting, not bed-pooping. But it worked perfectly. After about nine weeks of training with it, I was cured. We went out to Spiro›s, my favorite restaurant, that night to celebrate. For the first time in my life, at age 10, I was finally free of diapers.

Despite this triumph, the camp directors were nervous to have me. They were scared about all my physical problems and what a hassle they might be or how they might affect the other campers. What if I got exposed to latex there and had some crazy allergic reaction? They were also scared of a lawsuit. Their fears were totally reasonable, looking back on it. But my parents were unstoppable.

I was unaware of it at the time, but my parents fought the camp. They went to our temple to get members to lobby for me. In the end, the camp gave in. The camp directors arranged for me to use a nurse›s office to poop so that I had my privacy and avoided disturbing the other kids. After fighting so hard just to get the chance to go, camp itself was pretty easy.

These are a few of the many examples I could give of how competently and confidently my parents addressed my medical problems. I could have had a traumatic childhood. But their interventions, love, patience and kindness allowed me to live the life of a somewhat normal kid. I had no idea how much stress it was causing my parents until much later. All I was aware of was that I was encouraged in every way imaginable to think of problems as bumps in the road, rather than impassable roadblocks. Whatever it was costing my parents internally, they never let me think that running into an obstacle meant you just surrendered and accepted defeat.

Instead of being an unhappy kid, I was a fighter, a survivor who simply had a lot of issues. Dr. T and my parents had taught me this incredible ability to pursue my desires even while all of this embarrassing stuff was going on with my body. Through all the many years of problems, I never felt like the kid in the plastic bubble, living a completely isolated, weird life. Thank God they gave me such a good perspective. Because it was all going to get tested more and more severely as time went on.

I was five when I started blinking and rolling my eyes. I remember being in first grade and looking in the mirror. My eyes seemed to move around on their own, looking way up to the left and then way up to the right, circling around, opening and closing. It sounds strange, but I didn't really think anything of it at first. It set in so slowly. It crept up on me like a stalker.

I started to sniff. I'd blow these quick blasts of air out my nose. Like an animal in a cartoon, sneezing in a very comical, exaggerated way.

I remember Brian, my older brother, trying to help me stop. Four years older than me, he was generally very patient, but I'm sure there must have been times when my hovering around him, sniffing constantly, drove him nuts. By this, I don't mean I sniffed in; I wasn't inhaling. I was blasting air out of my nose, and often, I'd get little bits of snot on him. One day, he made me some little contraption out of construction paper and tape that was supposed to fit over my nose. He taped it on me, like a dog muzzle. It wasn't like he pinned me down and did it to be mean. He was actually trying to help, but it was horrible. It was summertime. I couldn't breathe, and I just sat there, feeling stupid.

My brother Justin was born when I was seven. Everyone was a bit distracted by him. He had such fuzzy hair and was so cute. I asked my parents if I could "pet him." Once when I was holding him, he threw up on me. I was so shocked, I dropped him. I think his presence in the house added a badly needed degree of normalcy. For a while, at least.

It didn't last long, however. Over the next few months, I started saying weird things. I had always been a polite kid. Anytime I burped, I would say "excuse me." But I started saying "excuse me" even if no one else was around. I started to say it way too often and for no reason.

I started to say "I love you." First it was just sometimes, and then it was more and more often. I'd walk around saying, "Excuse me, excuse me, excuse me. I love you, I love you, I love you." My friends and family thought it was cute. It was wonderful! And then suddenly, it was just bizarre. I couldn't stop.

I started trying to mask my weird speech habits by adding things to whatever I was saying or pretending like I was singing something intentional. "I love you" would become "I love you....r.. way of doing that thing when you put the ladder by the house!! La la la la la." I would be in a van full of kids, coming home from some sports activity or something, and I would be in the back singing along, going, "ah la la la la la la," to cover up whatever it was I'd just said.

The frequency of these habits went up and down. Sometimes they happened a lot. Sometimes I'd catch a break, and it would all settle down. The variation made it harder to realize what was going on. Early on, I don't remember anyone freaking out or being concerned. No one stopped me and said, "Marc, what are you doing?"

I don't know if it's real or if it's just an urban legend, but there's a pseudo-scientific study I've heard people quote quite often about how if you put a frog in a pot of water and slowly heat it up to a boil, the frog will never jump out because the change is so gradual. The poor frog simply doesn't notice that the water is getting hotter and that it's going to die. Looking back, that's how I view my Tourette's. It was this gradual progression. It evolved very slowly. And it was such a small thing compared to my other, more dramatic, health issues.

At the same time I was saying all these weird things, I was also becoming an extremely insistent, willful kid. Still cute and nice and likeable, but weirdly demanding and obsessive sometimes in a way that could come across as aggressive.

The person I antagonized the most throughout my life was my brother Brian.

Brian was an extremely well-behaved, intelligent kid. He was a bit nerdy, with huge round glasses, but overall very talented and accomplished. He always got top grades. He was chosen by a talent agency to act in commercials. He was a serious, earnest kid.

Our family room had these two huge blue pillows that Brian and I would throw on the floor so we could plop down and watch TV. The pillows were actually kind of disgusting. Every house seems to have them: They're never washed, and they probably have years of saliva from all the naps people have taken on them. But they're everyone's favorite. I would always come in and commandeer his pillow, even though he was there first. I'd just storm in and sit on it. I would do all this annoying stuff like that – not just once, but a million times.

I was always wreaking havoc. Our house wasn't particularly big, so we didn't have that many trash cans, but somehow it always became a big deal whenever our parents told us to empty the trash. One of us was supposed to be the dumper and dump the trash into a bag, and the other one was the holder, who held the bag. For some reason, we both felt that being the dumper was disgusting. Holding the bag was an executive position of great importance. It had to be done exactly right. If not, then the trash would pour out onto the ground, and the dumper would have to pick it up.

We had enormous fights about it. Who was going to dump the trash? Not me! Not me! Every Sunday night, or whenever it was trash time, our house turned into World War III. I was the one who usually got punished for it because I was the one who made the biggest ruckus. My dad would spank me. Brian never got spanked. Looking back, it's really sad that we turned this simple chore into a nightmare. Some of this was just regular sibling rivalry. But a lot of it was me.

Whenever I acted like a monster, my parents would tell Brian, "Rise above it, Brian. Rise above it." It was a mantra. They said it over and over. To his credit, most of the time, he did just that: He rose above it. He was an awesome brother. But sometimes, he would lose his temper. I remember one time he was standing on top of the steps, shrieking at me that I was robbing him of his happiness. And then he shouted, "I WISH YOU WERE DEAD!!" Our mother was livid. More likely, she was heartbroken but didn't know any other way to express her hurt than in anger. Imagine fighting so hard, for so many years, to keep one of your kids alive and then hearing the other one shout, "I wish you were dead!"

To a certain but very significant extent, my health issues became the center of our family's universe. There was a constant war for my parents' attention. And my medical needs and my insistent nature would always trump Brian's meeker, gentler personality. My parents tried very hard, but my brother got shafted. For Justin, it was easier because, by the time he came along, the sense of stress about my disorders was simply the status quo. But, as my dad says, Brian basically lost his parents when I was born. He was born into a normal family. And then suddenly, when I was born, my parents were thrust into emergency overdrive, going back and forth to the hospital all the time for my Hirschsprung's, then dealing with my odd behaviors. It altered our family chemistry forever.

My dad recalls that, when I had emergencies and Mom had to take me to the hospital, Brian would often get sick and throw up. It wasn't like he was faking. He really was throwing up. But our dad always suspected it was Brian's body's way of getting the attention he was missing out on.

My mom tried hard to balance it out. She used to have "special days" with Brian. She would spend the whole day with Brian, taking him somewhere cool, making sure that he got something closer to his fair share of the attention. But still, I was so demanding. I never let up.

We ended up going to a lot of counseling as a family because of my behavior. This started when I was five. And throughout those years, my parents just kept saying, "Rise above it, Brian. Rise above it." But Brian wasn't really the problem: The therapist advised my parents to study a book called *How to Tame the Strong-Willed Child.*

All of this was very frustrating to my parents because no one had any idea what was driving my behavior. I'm sure that, in their heads, they must have thought life wasn't fair. Why did one kid have to end up being so ridiculously high-maintenance?

When I was in third grade and Brian was in seventh, he had his bar mitzvah (A bar mitzvah – or bat mitzvah for girls – is a Jewish coming of age ceremony). By the time of the ceremony, my head had begun jerking back and forth, and my arms would flop around with a mind of their own. My parents were freaked out. My grandma felt bad for me. She felt bad for my parents. And she felt bad for Brian. Here it was, his moment to shine, but I was jigging around like a rag doll, distracting everyone. No one knew yet that Tourette's was making me act this way, so everything I was doing seemed like it must be on purpose or neurotic or emotional or somehow just weird. It was a mess! But, at the same time, it was an important, serious ceremony – it was Brian's entrance into manhood – so everyone tried to keep things together.

I barely remember this because I was still just a kid. But my grandma told me later how Dr. T came to the temple. This, in itself, was kind of amazing because she probably had a dozen kids to be saving that day. But like I said, ever since I was a baby, we called her my "other mother." She felt very much like a full-on member of the family.

My grandmother cried when she told me this story. She knew all the problems my disorders were causing for the family. And I think it made it that much sadder, or maybe that much more pronounced, to have had in Dr. T a witness to the events.

Dr. T insisted that she couldn't stay past the ceremony. As she was leaving the synagogue for the parking lot, she remembered she had brought a gift for my brother. My grandmother offered to walk Dr. T to her car. On the way, Dr. T, reflecting on the tensions she had noticed inside the temple, said to my grandmother, "You have a very unusual family." It was a compliment. It was her way of saying, "You guys are doing a good job of coping with so much stress."

My grandmother responded: "You're a very unusual doctor." And suddenly, they grabbed each other and sobbed.

When I was nine, my dad read an Ann Landers article about Tourette's. Until then, it hadn't occurred to anyone that my symptoms might be more than just nervous tics and willfulness. We made an appointment with a neurologist. Why not? It couldn't hurt. The neurologist confirmed my father's suspicion. And, although my symptoms didn't change at all from the day before that diagnosis to the day after, the news devastated my parents. I had just gotten out of diapers. I'd already had enough medical trauma. What was this going to mean? Somehow, getting an official diagnosis created a lot more stress.

I won't go into a prolonged scientific explanation of Tourette's, but the short version is that there are an estimated 200,000 people in the United States who have it. People tend to think of it as an incredibly rare disorder, but that number translates into about one or two people with Tourette's in every high school across America.

Tourette's is a neurological genetic disorder that alters chemical activity in the brain. Scientists don't know for sure, but they think Tourette's involves the neurotransmitter dopamine, a hormone that affects all sorts of important body functions like movement, attention and sleep.

You don't always know who has Tourette's because every case is so different. Some people learn to suppress their disorder so that it's barely noticeable. Some people have really subtle, manageable cases, and the ways in which the disorder manifests are unnoticed. Others have really, really obvious signs. Some people grow out of Tourette's by adolescence; some people are stuck with it for life.

For me, the disorder causes me to experience jolts of excess energy. Think of it like a power surge. Inside of me. Imagine taking a 40-watt bulb and zapping it with 100 watts of electricity. Imagine that happening in a human brain. The surge has to be released somehow. And the way it releases in me is in the form of a tic.

A tic is a movement or sound in reaction to that electrical surge. It's like a spasm, or a jerk. My blinks and the weird things I say – those are tics. There are many, many different kinds of tics that manifest in different Tourette's sufferers. One girl I knew of had a habit of jabbing her shoulder into her neck. She just had to do it. She eventually broke her neck because of the force of her shoulder jabbing so many times. She had another tic that made her inhale really quickly. Sometimes, she would do it so intensely, she would pass out.

Another kid I met later had convulsions several times a day that would last for as long as 45 minutes. Imagine this huge guy – he's about 6 feet 2 inches – having a full-out, violent convulsion. When other kids turn 16, they get their driver's license and start driving. When he turned 16, authorities told him, "No way." They were too afraid he'd seize up behind the wheel. (Eventually, he started getting Botox injections, which lessened his attacks to once every few weeks.)

Over the years, I have manifested, or displayed, many different tics. I would get one where I would suck in my stomach muscles until they hurt. I've also had itches in my jaw that made me clench my TMJ (the joint and muscle that runs from the chin to the ear) until it hurt. With another tic, I started to make a barking sound, almost like a dog. "Arp!" That's what it sounded like.

So this is what goes on *outside* my body. But the way a tic manifests *inside* me is like an itch. I might feel this itch in my brain or all over my body or inside specific parts of my body. I have no control over it; it just hits me. And when I tic, it's a response to feeling that itch. It's an attempt to scratch it, to get rid of it, to make it go away. While it's going on, the feeling is welling up inside me, creating physical tension, and I can't think about anything else but making it go away.

When an itch hits me, there's nothing I can do about it. It's completely involuntary. What happens after that – the scratch, let's call it – is semi-voluntary. In other words, I have some control over it. But not much.

A friend of mine who also has Tourette's gave me a great way to think about it. "Open up your eyes really wide," he said, "And don't blink until you start to feel the burning sensation."

Imagine yourself holding your eyes open. Sure, you can postpone blinking. For a while. But the longer you postpone it, the more it hurts. You have no control over the pain or the intensity. And eventually, you're going to have to blink. That's what's my Tourette's itches are like, and that's what's going on inside my body, all over my body, a lot of the time. Whether I have a little bit of control or none at all, it is incredibly, incredibly difficult, and virtually impossible, for me not to scratch my itches.

The easiest tic to explain is the one where I chomp my teeth. I feel this intense itchiness. I describe it as an invisible aura, like a ball of energy around my teeth. And suddenly, there's a feeling in my mouth saying, "Marc, you need to chomp your teeth in a certain way and with a certain intensity in order for this to go away." When I do, you can hear my teeth clicking loudly. Sometimes I want to chomp my teeth every few seconds. Sometimes I might not do it for minutes or even a half hour. When I sleep, I don't tic at all.

What was so bewildering as the Tourette's set in was that we never knew what was coming next. My mom and dad joked that we'd joined "the tic of the month club." Old ones would disappear, then return, then disappear again. New ones came every few weeks or months.

In middle school, I loved the theater. Luckily, my ticcing didn't keep me from getting cast in school plays and musicals. Interestingly, when I was focused on something intensely for short amounts of time, like acting in a scene, my Tourette's took a break. In sixth grade, I got cast in this play with a lot of seventh and eighth graders, which was pretty cool. Not only did I get to be in the play and not only did I get to hang out with the older kids, but I had a gigantic crush on this eighth grader named Katherine. She was so hot. Naturally, I kept trying to impress her.

One day I was at play practice, and we were between readings. I was lying on a table, resting, and I apparently ticced in some way that made me thrust my hips. I guess I was unconsciously humping the air a bit. This one girl came up to me afterward and said with a big smirk, "Hey, Marc! Looks like you had a really fun play practice!" Later I found out there was a rumor going around that I had been masturbating during play practice. I was horrified. (So much for winning over Katherine!)

By eighth grade, I was trying to hold back most of my tics. It was excruciating. I would come home after school and explode like the Tasmanian Devil, unleashing all the tics I'd suppressed all day while my mom watched, trying not to freak out.

In fact, if my parents hadn't informed them, most of my teachers would have had no idea that I had Tourette's. I did such a good job of suppressing the tics, hiding them, camouflaging them. Meanwhile, in the safety of my own home, I let them all hang out. I developed this one long-running tic in my neck, which was really painful. I would thrash my head to the right and then forcefully slash it back to the left, and just shake, shake, shake. It was like a dance move — this insanely violent, quick jerking. The less-violent but constant tics, like the sniffing, the barking, and the tooth-chomping, continued getting worse all the time.

Sometime during the summer after ninth grade, the coprolalia set in. I remember the first time it hit me. I had gotten my license by then, so I was driving along, singing out loud to R. Kelly's "The World's Greatest." Whenever he sang the words "I am an eagle," it sounded like he was singing, "I am a neagle." So I was singing along and all of a sudden, out of nowhere, I went from singing "I am a neagle" to "I am a nigger!" I was shocked. It was ridiculous and strange. Where did this come from? It didn't come from inside me. I wasn't someone who talked like that. Everyone knows the n-word is the worst word in the English language. What was I doing saying that word?

And then it kind of sunk in. Oh. Yeah. A tic. A new tic. By that time, I had seen so many strange tics creep up on me. I never saw them coming. Sometimes they cycled out of me and went away. But usually they came and stayed. And I would be stuck with them.

Within seconds of that strange utterance, I started to feel really sad. It wasn't like I suddenly started saying the n-word all the time. It took awhile. During that time, I started saying all kinds of other offensive, inappropriate things as well. Soon, I was saying not only the n-word, but a whole long list of offensive words like "pussy," "jack-off," "boring," "fat!" I was constantly appalled at myself. Friends and family were shocked. Even when they understood that it was not me, but my Tourette's, it was hard for them to handle sometimes.

There were times when I'd be with friends and I'd say something horrible in a public place or in a social setting. My friends would say, "Really? Do you have to say that?" And I would cringe. What could I say? I wanted to die sometimes – or at least be invisible.

No one in my family swore much. We weren't like that. Always, always, I had been the polite kid, the kid who incessantly said thanks to my friends' parents when I ate at their homes or to whoever had driven me somewhere in a car pool. So many kids had this entitlement thing, and they treated their friends' parents like servants. Not me. But, all of a sudden, I was saying to adults things like "hairy thong!"

I learned that about 10 percent of people with Tourette's suffer from coprolalia. And I had become one of them. I learned that there was no word I wouldn't say and no one whose feelings I couldn't offend. I mentioned earlier that my older brother and I fought sometimes, but he was also my best friend and idol. He really was. Yet constantly, I ticced "Faggot!" and "You're gay!" to him, over and over. My brother Justin, six years younger, was growing up in a house full of swear words and weird utterances coming out of my mouth. Besides swear words, I said things like "I hate you" to my father sometimes. Sometimes I said it out of anger, and maybe I was just being a brat, but oftentimes, it was the Tourette's. It was very hard for anyone to know where Marc left off and the Tourette's began. I wasn't even sure myself sometimes.

I started trying to confuse people by saying these things quietly, or rushing my words, or cramming other words into my speech to cover up what I was saying. I might add "dad" after saying the n-word so that it would come out "niggerdad!" It confused people a little bit, maybe, but it was still extremely awkward. I also became hyperaware of my behavior. If I started to tic the n-word while reading a book in public, for example, I'd continue reading as if nothing had happened. If someone heard me and looked in my direction, they'd see a kid who wasn't doing anything wrong. I hoped – often correctly – they'd question their own judgment and decide they had misheard me.

Sometimes I would try to step out of my body and look at myself through other people's eyes. It was a really bad place to go. There was nothing fun about imagining people looking at me, watching me chomping my teeth, biting the air and barking. Far worse was when I imagined the effects of my words – "nigger" and all the other offensive things I was beginning to say – on other people.

It wasn't flattering, fun or comfortable. When I thought about it, I could see how people would judge me. Here I was, saying all these things that caused other people pain and discomfort. I had no intention of hurting anyone. I'm not a racist. I understand that African-Americans have suffered greatly in the United States and that racism is still an enormous issue and that every time I ticced the n-word, I was creating pain. I felt just like Edward Scissorhands sometimes. There was so little I could do about it. What were my choices? I developed three techniques for covering my offenses: confidence, humor and flat-out denial. When in doubt, make a joke or repress and press on. I'm not saying this was right or good or the best choice, but it's the best choice I could make at that age.

Tourette's is known as a co-morbid disorder. If you have it, you are very likely to have one or more of these other disorders as well: ADHD, ADD, depression, social anxiety and even bipolarity. They all stem from the same part of the brain. Eventually, I was diagnosed with OCD – obsessive compulsive disorder.

We learned that my particular combination of OCD and Tourette's interacted in a way that produced a constant desire to seek out the riskiest behavior in any given environment. When I was in elementary school, I had incredibly intense urges to put my hand down the garbage disposal – while it was running. It was an itch, just like my other tics. I'd be at the sink, cleaning the plates, and I would suddenly have this strong compulsion to put my hand down through the hole, past the rubber trap, toward the blade. The disposal would be running, and, as my hand went down, it felt good. I wouldn't put my hand in all the way to the running blades, but I'd come awfully close. Believe me: I love my fingers. But I just had to "scratch" that OCD-driven itch.

As I got older, this kind of behavior became more common. When we went on a family trip to Chicago and visited the Sears Tower observation deck, I felt compelled to go to the edge of the building and get up on the railing. This wasn't something I thought about. It was a compulsion, like my other itches. I felt a tremendous temptation to hoist myself over the edge a bit, just to feel my center of gravity tipping over the side. This need to push the edge resurfaced over and over. When I would ride a bike, I would let go of the handle and see how far I could go before the bike tipped over. Later on, when riding on the back of a friend's motorcycle, I had a strong urge to let go and feel my body hit the pavement.

My goal was to reach the edge of that feeling of nearly losing control. I didn't actually want to get there – I just wanted to get close. This was my OCD. It was at the root of what my parents referred to as my willfulness. It was responsible for my urge to say offensive things. It was all OCD, pulling the strings, compelling me toward actions over which I had little control.

It's important to stress that, regardless of what my tics looked like, they were completely unrelated to my thoughts and emotions. Whether I was saying the n-word in front of a black person, blurting out "you're gay" to someone acting effeminately, or pursuing risky behavior like putting my hand down the disposal, I wasn't doing these things because I hated other people or hated myself. I was responding to neurological quirks inside my brain.

Although my tics were in no way *caused* by emotional problems, it was obvious that they were *causing* me to suffer emotionally. Everyone knows that adolescence is a period of intense stress and sensitivity. My body was going through the normal adolescent changes, which were already painful enough. But when I looked in the mirror and saw myself, I found it hard not to wonder what was happening and where this disorder was taking me.

Somewhere around this time, my parents took me to see a psychologist. His son had suffered a serious brain injury, and the doctor had done a lot of work and research to try to help his son. He had even developed his own neuro-bio feedback technology to teach his son to regain control over his brain. When I visited the psychologist, he attached a series of electrodes to monitor my brain activity. The idea was that he was going to train me to relax my brain.

We sat there watching my indicators on a computer monitor. There was this sort of chart, or graph thing, measuring my stress level. When my stress went up and my breathing tightened up, the indicators would jump, and I would see spikes in the graph. When I relaxed and calmed down and breathed more deeply, the spikes would be smaller. Every time I ticced, the stress level jumped way up.

This exercise was supposed to teach me to be aware of the rise and fall of my stress level. After every tic, and every jump in stress level, I was supposed to consciously step back and allow my breathing to relax and my whole body to calm. Relax. Relax.

I went for five sessions. Every time, we worked on getting me to relax. And every time I left, I would forget everything I learned in exactly two seconds. I would tic. I would stress out. I would panic. That was my constant state of mind. I didn't have the concentration. I couldn't. And I was so used to that level of stress, it was normal for me. How do you tell a ninth grader to find his Zen every moment of the day? It wasn't like I was resisting the guy. I just couldn't relax.

I was playing sports. I was totally girl-crazy. I had friends. I worked hard in school. Big parts of my life were normal and happy.

But let's face it: I'd won a pretty horrible lottery. Odds of having Tourette's are 1 in 200,000. Odds of having Hirschsprung's are 1 in 5,000. Multiply the two and figure it out: odds of being me and having my particular medical challenges were one in a billion. I may have had the disposition to be a normal kid, but the fact was, life was throwing a lot of lightning bolts at me. It was stressful, and the storm wasn't even over yet.

I'll never forget this: At one point during our sessions, the psychologist looked at me and said, "Kid, you know what? If you were 40 years old and you had this level of stress, you'd be dead."

I'm going to go into an aspect of my problems so central to my story, I can't conceal it. The short version is that, because of my Hirschsprung's, my Tourette's, and my OCD combined, I developed weird issues around defecating – or pooping.

I mentioned that my bowel movements had always been liquid. Only liquid. Every time. But when I was about eight or nine years old, my Tourette's and OCD came along and messed me up even more. I became obsessive about pooping, just like I was about so many other things. I began to feel like I constantly had to empty myself, to get rid of any poop that was inside me. It was just another tic: I seldom had control over it. If I had any fecal matter inside, I was likely to feel the urge to poop it out. If I was exercising at the gym, waiting for a bus, driving a car, whatever – I wanted to expel whatever was inside me.

Along the way, I developed an obsessive-compulsive way of pooping. If you've ever had air trapped in your stomach and tried to make yourself burp to get rid of it, imagine instead that you just keep sucking up more air. You sit there sucking in air, then burping it out, then sucking it up again, just trying to get back to normal. You don't want to feel like something is stuck inside you. That's how I felt about pooping. It's hard to describe, but somehow I learned to suck air into my butt-hole and then blast it out again.

I've never heard anyone poop as loud as me. Imagine this combination of air being sucked in, and air and liquid coming out: It almost sounds like a whoopee cushion. It's the most ridiculous amount of noise anyone has ever made pooping. Even with a bathroom door shut and a fan on, you can hear the noise from many feet away.

Can you think of anything more embarrassing for a kid? Think about how few people ever took a poop in elementary school. No one wants to poop around their peers! Even as people get older, if they use the bathroom at a friend's house and there's someone in the next room, they often turn on the sink, the fan or pee on the side of the toilet bowl to cover up the noise they make.

So imagine the shame of making a huge amount of noise every time you poop and having to do it up to eight times a day. I was so embarrassed. For years, it was a constant source of humiliation – much worse than the Tourette's. Every day of my life was an immersion in total shame.

I would do anything to hide my problem. If I was in a bathroom stall at a restaurant, with no noise barriers, and someone else came in, I would stop what I was doing and wait until they left. I would try to sneak in a blast while someone turned on the sink or when they hit the fan to dry their hands. If several people were coming in and out, I'd be there forever, waiting to be alone. Sometimes it would take me 20 minutes to take a crap.

I assumed everyone was repulsed by me and my noises. How could they not be? All I could see were their ankles and shoes. But I knew what they must be thinking: I was weird or disgusting. If they could see me, I was sure they would laugh at me. Every time I sat desperately in one of those stalls, I would think to myself: "Why can't these people just let me be!!? Why can't I just take a poop in peace like a normal person?"

It became a logistical nightmare, constantly trying to figure out a safe and nearby place to poop. I felt vulnerable all the time.

From the beginning, my parents were so resourceful about dealing with my challenges that, in my eyes, they were – and remain – truly heroic. They never made me feel like I wasn't a "normal" child. They never made me feel guilty for the burdens I continually added to the family. My challenges were a fact of life. There was no shame about them.

My parents' primary interest had always been their kids, but the sheer enormity of dealing with me and my disorders had created a lot of tension in their marriage. They had always been very social, and they had a lot of friends, but they never had time for things like hobbies. They had had to harness their energies and direct them in a way that most families don't. I can tell you about family trips and vacations that were ruined because of my disorders – trips we had to cut short, trips we had to cancel.

When I was a teenager, my parents went to a marriage counselor who warned them that something like 80 percent of parents of critically ill children ended up getting divorced. When I was 21, after 30 years of marriage, that's what they did. They turned out to be as human as everyone else.

I don't blame myself for their divorce. There were other problems besides me. But I try to imagine what it must have been like for them to have to deal with a kid like me. I will never stop feeling like they did an amazing job of coping.

My parents were the ones who first showed me how to be open and gracious about my challenges when I was in public. One night when I was in sixth grade, we were at a restaurant. People at the table next to us were getting upset by my tics. To my total surprise, my father rose and handed them a little card he had printed up. He'd gotten it from the Tourette Syndrome Association. At the top, the card said, "WHY DO I ACT THIS WAY?" and then it went on to explain about Tourette's. The best part about the description was the last line: "I'm sorry if bothers you. It bothers me more."

Not only did my father's actions and that little card solve the problem, but the family who had been so disturbed by my tics got genuinely curious and started asking us questions to learn more. We ended up sitting with them and having a great conversation.

I began to carry the cards around with me. Whenever it seemed like a good idea, I would hand them out to people. It was a huge step for me. I had never had much choice about hiding or not hiding a lot of my challenges. But here was a way of being open about my Tourette's that was much smarter and more comfortable than any method I could have devised on my own. It was more comfortable for me and probably for most people around me. Instead of feeling awkward and trying to pretend like everything was normal and fine, why not be open? Why not bridge the gap between my suffering and other people's confusion? It was a nice way to bring people into my life.

I think this kind of forwardness about my problems, and what I would later learn to call advocacy, made for an easier time in high school than I would have had if I hadn't reached out to teachers and fellow students to explain my situation. Everyone knew about my Tourette's, and most people accepted it. (Almost no one knew about my Hirschsprung's because the school arranged for me to use a private bathroom in the nurse's office. I was adept at scooting in there like a toilet ninja and taking care of business without anyone knowing. Few people knew about my noisy poops, and people thought of me simply as a guy with Tourette's. Fine by me.)

Ironically, there were some silver linings that came along with Tourette's. Swearing and talking dirty were such big deals for most kids. My Tourette's gave me a free pass to swear all the time.

Among the movies and books out there that depict what Tourette's is like, there's a Hallmark special about a guy, also from St. Louis, who eventually becomes a well-regarded teacher. Of course, there are documentaries and websites and news programs that have discussed the issue. But one of the best-known depictions of Tourette's comes from the Comedy Central show "South Park."

For anyone who doesn't know, "South Park" is an animated series that's very irreverent, very dirty and very funny. In one storyline, the character Cartman sees a kid in a toy store shouting obscenities in full view of his mother. Cartman is immediately intrigued because, in a show full of obscenities and swear words, he is by far the most foul-mouthed and aggressive. Cartman becomes very curious. How in the world does this kid have permission to swear and shout and be foul-mouthed in public? In front of his mother, no less? He learns from the kid's mom that the boy has this magical syndrome called Tourette's. Well, Cartman may have never heard of it before, but he knows a good thing when he sees it. By the next morning, he has Tourette's. He successfully cons everybody (except his friend Kyle, who instinctively knows he's faking) into thinking he's got it, and, for a while, it's great. He gets to mess with people's heads and swear in public!

What's so funny about this storyline is how often it works out to be true. There were times that my Tourette's allowed me to get away with murder.

On the first day of sophomore year of high school, I walked into my Honors Algebra/Trig class. My teacher had given me permission to introduce myself so, before the lesson began, I stepped up front to explain about my Tourette's. The goal was to avoid freaking anybody out. But, of course, that didn't work out so well. I immediately started to yell "SEX! BREASTS! SEX!" Everybody started to laugh, including me. I could barely keep talking, "My name is Marc. I have SEX! Excuse me. SEX! Sorry, I have Tourette syndrome!"

Later that same year, in English class, each of us had to give a presentation. My best friend Greg stood at the podium in front of about 25 kids and began to recite a very romantic, serious poem. The whole class got quiet; we were all listening, being respectful. As he finished, there was this tiny pause, and I couldn't help it. I ticced: "You're gay." The whole class broke out laughing, including Greg and the teacher.

Another time, I was ticcing "F..k" in my Spanish class. The teacher looked at me and said, "Marcos, you can't say that in my class." I freaked out because she knew about my Tourette's. Then she said, "But if you do, it better be in Spanish!"

I had many people who, instead of being repelled by my Tourette's, were envious. My younger brother Justin told me that when he was younger half of his friends were jealous of my Tourette's because I could swear. He said he actually wished he had it sometimes because it gave me a personality. It gave me something to talk about. It was an icebreaker. It was funny and gave me something that made me stick out. Girls remembered me, and all my classmates knew who I was.

Of course, it wasn't so simple. I was in McDonald's once, and a guy came up to me and said, "Oh, my God, do you have Tourette syndrome?" I said, "Yeah." And he said, "Dude! That is so awesome." I sort of laughed and asked, "Really?" He said, "Yeah it is! You can say curse words! And it's cool, 'cause you have an excuse!!"

I thought for a second, wondering how to convey to a stranger what it's really like. I looked around the McDonald's and saw that there were some black customers and employees. I said, "OK. Do me a favor. I want you to say the 'n-word' as loud as you can right now."

He got the point pretty quickly: Anyone who ever thought Tourette's might be fun was looking at it in what I call a very "a la carte" kind of way, as if you can pick and choose which parts of the disorder you want and then leave the rest behind.

Sure, it might be funny to say "penis!!" in a class with a really strict teacher and make everyone break out laughing. But if you're saying these words and calling attention to yourself, and if you have to explain yourself all the time and hope that everyone understands and forgives you, it gets old. Very quickly. My disorder might be funny sometimes, but it's not something anyone would ever choose to live with all the time.

Let me give you some examples of the darker side. Once, when I was still in middle school, my dad and I went to see "We Were Soldiers," with Mel Gibson. My vocal tics had gotten pretty bad by that point, but we figured a movie about the Vietnam War would be loud. We figured we could handle it. We were wrong. In between the battle scenes, there were all these very quiet moments. In one scene, Mel and his wife were having this very deep, meaningful conversation; even though I was trying to hold back as much as I could, I couldn't help barking away. Out of nowhere, someone yelled, "Shut the fuck up!!!"

I felt so bad. I didn't go back to a movie theatre for almost a year. And then when I did, I would bring a washcloth. I would put it in my mouth and bite down. I still do this whenever I go to a movie.

When I was on sports teams and we had games, I'd have to go over to the opposing team's coach and explain myself and my Tourette's. I'd ask permission to make an announcement to his team and then, whether he gave permission or not, I'd go ahead and say what I needed to say.

When I was in 11th grade, we had a tennis match against a school called Kirkwood. As usual, I approached the opposing players to let them know about my Tourette's. We began to play. My own match ended early, so I decided to watch our number one player's match. As I stood on the fence surrounding the court, with a bunch of other people, my tics began to attract attention. To be honest, they were incredibly noticeable. But everyone had already been warned about them and I thought the issue was neutralized. Before I knew it, a dad came over and started yelling at me to leave the game. He happened to be the father of the Kirkwood player. He accused me of trying to sabotage the match. I defended myself, but he wouldn't let up. In the end, I backed away from the court to let the match continue.

Around the same time, I was waiting in line at Wendy's. There was this woman next to me. I was barking like a dog, doing my thing, and she started to giggle. I said, "Ma'am, my name is Marc Elliot. I have Tourette syndrome. I just want to let you know. I can't help it." She sort of laughed it off, like it was no big deal. About 10 seconds went by. All of a sudden, I heard her making an announcement to all of the workers behind the counter: "Guys, this here is Marc. Don't worry about him. He's just retarded." She wasn't teasing me or being mean. I think she was just trying to help. Retarded … Tourette's … whatever! What's the difference?

I'm not going to lie. In these situations where I felt people weren't tolerant of me, I got angry inside. There were so many times when people simply thought that I was joking or said, "Oh, come on, you don't have Tourette's." What was so aggravating was the fact that these people had no idea who I was and yet thought I was this horrible, annoying or uncaring person. If only they knew everything that I had done in my life, the plays, the student council I'd been elected to, they wouldn't think I was any of those things. They'd know I was more than the twitching, chomping, barking, swearing weirdo they saw. They would know I was a decent guy.

For anyone who hung out with me during these years, my disorders meant frequent social weirdness. Besides the fact that I constantly said inappropriate and offensive things out loud in public places, my behavior was also capable of creating confusion. I would sometimes start ticcing strangers' names again and again. Sometimes it was people I didn't even know, sometimes it was people I had just met. Sometimes, if I was in public and heard a family call out one of their kids' names, I would start ticcing that name. The kid would look at me, wondering what in the world I was doing. It was all a little Rain Man-y at times.

Sometimes people thought that what I I ticced reflected my subconscious thoughts about them. My friend Ranjit came up to me one day after a big party to tell me how drunk he'd gotten the night before, and I ticced, "alcoholic!" He was really ashamed and embarrassed because he thought that's what I thought of him.

My best friend Jodie once told me that the hardest thing about being my friend wasn't that I had Tourette's; it was that she never knew if it was the Tourette's or if I was just being a jerk! Of course, as a teenage kid, sometimes I *was* just being a jerk.

My disorders created tensions that went beyond my friends. My parents noticed that some parents were nervous, embarrassed, unsupportive or even unhappy about their kids being friends with me. Maybe they were worried my bad language was going to rub off on their kids.

For a while during ninth grade, which is maybe when people are at their most insecure, I did lose some friends because they just didn't know how to deal with me.

I had one really good friend named Adam Drucker. We'd been best friends since second grade. We always hung out at each other's houses. He'd seen my weird potty-training fire truck contraption in fourth grade and had actually slept over when I was using it. (It went off twice that night.) He was one of the few people close enough to me to know all about my issues. He knew my poops were loud. He'd seen my tics come. He'd been with me every step of the way as a real friend.

But in ninth grade, he suddenly stopped being there for me. He told me later that he just didn't know how to deal with me anymore. He shut me out without any warning. And then, very quietly and suddenly, a whole group of friends I'd been with forever withdrew their friendship.

One night I was at my house and I called these friends to see what they were up to. No one picked up the phone. That was unusual. It wasn't a total blackout, like everyone just dumped me. But they all became mysteriously distant, as if on cue, simultaneously. For a few weeks, at least, I felt like I was being shunned by this entire group of friends.

It didn't make sense to me – and it was scary. Friendship was so important in my life. My friends were everything.

My policy in life, both consciously and unconsciously, for good and for bad, was to plow right ahead. If there was doubt, insecurity or deviousness going on around me, I ignored it. If people weren't sure they wanted to be my friend, I pretended not to notice. It's not like I wasn't aware of what was happening. I understood why they were moving away from me. It stung. It stung a lot. But what choice did I have? I could be funny about the situation, I could ignore it, I could deny it, and I could talk about it. I remained open about my challenges, and whoever didn't like it didn't have to stick around. I'm sure I lost friends that way. Some people probably just got sick of me talking about my issues all the time. I even got sick of me talking about my issues all the time. During the worst of it, I felt like I was in a terrible downward spiral.

I talked with my principal about studying abroad sophomore year. It would have been so nice to leave, to exit, to disappear. I wanted to change my life somehow, to escape this feeling of social pressure. I was tired of not feeling accepted, of fighting to fit in. I was putting up such a façade, always trying to get people to like me despite my disorders. It was exhausting. I started asking my parents if I could switch to a private school.

After my freshman year, I changed high schools. This didn't have so much to do with my Tourette's, actually. My parents moved from one school district to a better one so my younger brother and I could get a better education. It seemed like a good idea at the time; in the end, it was a huge source of stress. At my old school, Parkway Central, I had known a lot of kids since grade school. At my new school in Clayton, I only knew one girl – my friend, Jodie. At my old school, my brother Brian, the rock star, the super-achiever, had paved the way for me. Everyone knew him and knew me as his little brother. We knew all the teachers and all the administrators, and they knew me and knew how to cope with my issues.

All that changed when I changed schools. We knew zero teachers, no administrators, and, in a school with 800 kids, I knew no one, other than Jodie. This truly was a coming-out party for my Tourette's. My stress level ballooned, which made my Tourette's get much worse, which then made me stress out even more. It was a vicious cycle.

It was traumatic. I felt like I had two choices: try to assimilate or become a relentless advocate for myself, even to the point of being a pain. I had been pretty open about my Tourette's, but this was a whole new ball game. I felt like I had to start all over again. Another round of persuading, introducing, explaining myself. Another round of minimizing people's discomfort, hoping and hoping they wouldn't hate me because I was weird. Another round of scoping out bathrooms. Another round of dealing with people's intolerance and teasing.

A lot of this was positive. My family met with administrators; we met with my teachers. Not only did I get a private bathroom set up for me, but every teacher agreed that I could make a short announcement before the first class got under way.

My first day at the new school was excruciating. I had thought the teachers would allow me to speak at the beginning of each class. But one teacher waited for 10 minutes before calling me up. Another completely forgot. Meantime, I was sitting there, ticcing, and all the kids were looking at me like, "What in the world is wrong with this disgusting weirdo?" I was getting sweaty and short of breath. I felt like I had a 50-pound weight on my chest. All I wanted to do was explain myself! I felt miserable and totally uncomfortable. And this was the first day of school!

Later on, when I was playing a JV soccer game, our team walked off the field past the varsity team. I don't remember exactly, but I think I was barking. I saw the varsity captain start to laugh. I had seen these guys around school, and, since they were on the varsity soccer team, they were considered cool. I wanted them to like me, but, obviously, we weren't getting off to a wonderful start.

I have no idea how I had the courage to do this. This wasn't the kind of thing that makes people like each other. But I knew I had to look out for myself. I went over to the coach and said, "Listen, your team captain was just laughing at me. I just thought you'd want to know." The coach went over and talked to the kid. They left me alone. It didn't help us get to be best friends, but I had to do it. I didn't feel like there was a better option.

Around the same time, I went to one of my favorite restaurants. I was sitting with a group of friends on a Sunday afternoon. My tics were bad; I was barking. After a while, I start to hear someone else making barking noises. I look over, and, a few tables away, there was a guy – an adult – sitting with two kids, mimicking me. He was about 35, this guy with two little kids, maybe four or five years old. He was mocking me, really loudly. I got up, walked over to him and said, "Hey man. I have Tourette syndrome. And I have never seen this in life. You're a role model for these kids, and you're teaching them that it's OK to make fun of other people?" The guy was stunned. He didn't say anything. I went back to my table. After a minute, he and his kids got up, put their trays away and walked out.

Now, that was NOT easy for me to do. I was completely nauseated with fear. But I was also determined to fight back, to not just take such humiliating treatment sitting down. I knew that if I had allowed the mocking to continue, I would have felt awful for, well, forever. But I was sweating. I was out of breath.

For three summers, I had worked at a camp for kids with cancer named Camp Rainbow. My experience as a counselor profoundly changed the way I looked at my own life. Three- fourths of the counselors were young, Jewish teenagers like me who didn't have cancer. Some of the counselors were cancer survivors. Brian had volunteered in the past, and I thought of the job as an honor. The night before the campers arrived, all the counselors who had survived their own struggle with cancer stood before us and told us their story. Two stories in particular still linger in my head today. The first came from a girl named Nikki, who was incredibly cute and bubbly. When she was seven, doctors found a tumor in her body that had become so elongated that it had wrapped itself around her lungs, heart and part of her left arm. Throughout her chemotherapy treatment, she had had constant acid reflux, which destroyed her throat. The hardest thing about the entire ordeal, she said, was one night in particular, when her mother sat next to her bed crying. Nikki recalled, "I just felt so bad for her to see me like this."

Another counselor named Henry shared his struggle. His life had been as normal as could be. Then, one day, he began to have vision problems. After a few doctors, it was discovered that Henry had a brain tumor and needed surgery – immediately. They rushed him to Children's Hospital, and although they were able to remove most of the tumor, part of it was inoperable. To this day, Henry lives with the tumor, which at any moment could resume its growth. I sat in my brown aluminum chair, listening to this story, ticcing as usual, and thinking about my intestinal disease. Even though I was crying from the stories and from my own pain, I couldn't help feeling lucky to be alive. I realized that my challenges might be tough, but a lot of people out there faced struggles far worse than mine.

As a result, I decided early on to look at my life as a blessing, not a curse. I was lucky to have survived, not unlucky to have problems. My job was to be happy, not to suffer.

For the most part, I've lived up to this decision. But it hasn't always been easy. I am sure that plenty of times, if I had been able to look fearlessly beneath my relentlessly positive attitude, I would have found some desperation and rage lurking around.

I had such a strong sense of right and wrong. I never wanted to let anyone push me around, and I always stuck up for other people who were getting pushed around. Believe it or not, despite the fact that I frequently said the word "fa..ot" and "gay," I always got upset when people used those words negatively. When I said them, it was without a negative intention. I repeatedly tried to talk people down from being verbally abusive. I guess that went along with standing up for myself.

Part of what drove me to be so open was I didn't want people to think I was a horrible person. I wanted people to understand that when I ticced something offensive, it wasn't intentional. The openness totally paid off. One time I was walking down the hallway, ticcing the n-word and this black kid stopped in his tracks, dumbfounded. From his point of view, it must have looked like I was deliberately taunting him. Just then, a female student, also black, passed by and saw what was happening. She touched the kid on the shoulder and said, "Oh, don't worry. That's Marc. He can't help it."

It didn't dawn on me until much later that I might be playing a positive role in other people's lives. Here I was, this skinny 16-year-old, stomping around, both ticing and explaining what was wrong with me, totally wearing my challenges on my sleeve. To me, this was my life. My telling people I had Tourette's had become as normal as saying my name.

One of my best friends, Ross, told me that I'd had a powerful effect on his mother, who suffered from muscular dystrophy. Her legs didn't work so well, and she walked with a limp. She had always been afraid to ask whomever she was with to slow down so she could keep up. After watching me and observing how hard I fought to get people to help me fit in, she was encouraged to speak up for herself. That was nice to hear.

While I put so much energy into presenting an outward appearance that my life was running crisply and smoothly, the reality was that I was always battling a grueling war within myself. It was just a fact of my life: On many levels, I was happy. But the basic fact was that an enormous part of my energy was spent trying either to curb my behavior, rein myself in, hold back or to appease, assuage, charm and make everyone laugh and feel at ease. I couldn't afford to have people not like me.

I know that, to a degree, everyone does this; it's called "people pleasing." But because of my challenges, I did it more. And I did it every day of my life. It was exhausting.

Even in high school, my life was still being affected by occasionally recurring health problems. Since being diagnosed with Tourette's, I had largely stayed away from medications. There wasn't much on the market that had been proven to be effective with any kind of guarantee. Toward the end of my junior year, however, my head-shaking got so bad that I was willing to try anything. I wanted a quick fix, to make it stop. But that's not how drugs to treat.Tourette's work. If there's any chance they are going to work, it takes time, trial and error, and luck. I sort of jumped into treatment and immediately experienced a weirdly treacherous interaction with the drug I was taking. I became extremely lethargic, and the medication triggered a chemically induced depression. I basically spent a whole month at home, playing video games. It was awful. Missing four weeks of school set me way back. After it was over and I had bounced back to normal, I remember sitting with my teachers and advisers at a conference table, discussing my fate. Should I plan on staying in high school for an extra year? The idea of taking a fifth year seemed shameful.

Like my brother had said, my Tourette's made me highly noticeable. I wouldn't say I was the most popular guy in high school, but I had come a long way since my first day in school. Three years after arriving, in my senior year, I ran for student body president. I still laugh about my campaign slogan: "Checkmark Marc," with a picture of a checkmark. It was kind of making fun of my Tourette's, like a tic. Ha ha. Except I won.

This was a typical kind of story for me . I was never some isolated guy who didn't get to participate in life. I never felt like, "Oh no, I don't get to be part of the human race." It was more like, "OK, I can be part of the human race. But it's always going to be a little trickier for me." Despite my stresses and all the things I'm writing about here, I was more or less a successful high school student. But…. The "buts" kept happening, too.

One night, I went to a Japanese restaurant with a group of about a dozen friends. It was a surprise birthday party for my friend Jossie. The restaurant was super quiet and small. After we arrived, I went around to the other tables, maybe about four or five of them, and said, "Hey, my name is Marc. I've got Tourette syndrome." Then I went on with my spiel.

I sat down, and everything was fine. Then, all of a sudden, this guy approached our table. He was maybe 25 years old, skinny, tall, white with brown hair. He looked like he'd had a few beers. He leered at me and said, "I might be a South County hick" – South County was a rural area near St. Louis – "but I'm no idiot. If you don't stop making those noises, I'm gonna beat the crap out of you."

We were stunned. My friend Richard was sitting next to me. He went stone cold, he was so shocked. That was the first threat against me that he or anyone else at the table had seen before. They – and I – saw what could happen outside of our controlled school environment.

I stood up, thinking, "I'll just reason with him. People are nice. He'll understand once I explain myself." So I put my hand out and tried to show him my medical bracelet, which explained my Tourette's and blah blah. I was babbling away, doing my thing, when suddenly he grabbed my wrist. He looked crazy and angry. I thought he was going to kick the crap out of me. Luckily, one of my friends came over to help, and I guess the man realized he was outnumbered. He dropped my arm and walked away. The situation was defused. But right at that moment, while we were still standing there and still shocked, the girl whose birthday it was came in. What could we say? "Ummm, surprise!!" The whole thing was totally ruined.

That kind of episode would happen every once in a while, but it never had such an impact on me that I thought, "Oh, I need to change my life. This absolutely has to be addressed." But then the Greyhound bus incident happened.

It was August 11, 2002 – the day before my 17th birthday. My friend, Jodie, and four other friends were going to a Jewish sleep-away camp in Indianapolis. I had never been there before, so I was totally excited. Jodie had this idea of taking a Greyhound bus to and from St. Louis. We thought it would be a fun adventure.

On the ride to the Greyhound station, I started to get a little nervous. My Tourette's was very, very bad at the time, and pretty much whenever I saw black people or people who were gay, short, obese or had birth defects, I would begin to tic – "Nigger!," "Faggot!," "Short!" "Fat!" and so on – whatever was the worst possible name to call them.

To my relief, the bus was almost empty. There was one black guy, sitting a few rows ahead of us. I told him I had Tourette's as soon as I got on, and he seemed fine. I probably said "nigger" a few times, but either he didn't hear or he understood and accepted it. Nothing bad happened, and five hours later, we were in Indianapolis. Thank God.

Camp was great. But I should qualify what I mean by "great." My Tourette's meant, for example, that there were moments when

we'd be having religious services, and everyone would be silent –
except me. I'd be barking and sniffing and distracting everyone. My
Tourette's meant that, whenever I saw this girl whom I had a crush
on, I would begin to tic "Michelle's muff, Michelle's muff, Michelle's
muff." Not exactly the best way to make an impression.

My Tourette's meant that one night, when we were all sitting in a
discussion group by the campfire, I kept ticcing "mole, mole, mole."
In the group was a girl with a mole. I couldn't stop saying it. It was so
humiliating. I literally had to run away. I couldn't stop myself.

My Tourette's meant that, on our last night of camp, three friends
of mine did a rap, making fun of my disorder. They rapped to this
song by Ludacris and Jermaine Dupri called "Welcome to Atlanta."
They kept doing this one gesture that mimicked one of my tics. It was
funny, yes, but it also reminded me of how much I stood out.

So when I say camp was great, it has to be understood in this
qualified way. It was fun, but it was complicated.

I was still buzzing from camp when we walked into the Greyhound station in Indianapolis. It hit me right away: "We're going to
have a problem."

The Greyhound station in Indianapolis is a huge, cavernous place
with columns. It wasn't packed, exactly, but most of the people there
were black. I didn't know this at the time, but Indianapolis, it turns
out, used to have a very active Ku Klux Klan chapter, all the way up
through the 1990s. Racial tensions were even higher there than they
were in a lot of other places. So imagine: We walk in, I see all these
black people, and, immediately, I start ticcing "nigger."

We hung out for a minute, trying to figure out where to go. I saw
a security guard and to be on the safe side I went over to tell him that
had Tourette's. He just shrugged, like "Whatever, OK."

A few minutes later, we were standing in line, a black woman in
front of me. I started ticcing: "nigger" "nigger." The woman turned
around and gave me a look. I apologized and gave her one of my
cards explaining about Tourette's.

I don't know if she thought I was mentally unstable or if she
thought I was trying to sell her something or if she was just so of-
fended, but she refused to read the card. I gave it to this huge guy I assumed was her boyfriend, and he read it. But he didn't say much. He
just handed it back to me with a neutral look on his face. I had no idea
if things were OK or if they were escalating or what. It was just tense.

We boarded the bus, and, as we passed the driver, I gave her one of my cards. She looked it over and said, "Don't worry about it." We took our seats, and I looked around. Except for two white hippies, it was me and my friends – six Jewish kids – and the rest of the bus, which was entirely black and totally packed.

I had asked the bus driver to make an announcement, which is something I've learned to do on airplane flights, as well. (I usually ask flight attendants to read something to calm people down.) So when the driver started to indicate the exits and the bathrooms and say all the normal procedural stuff, she added, "I also want to let everyone know that there's a young man on this bus who has Tourette syndrome. It could be great if we could all be a little understanding."

I got up and did a little Miss America wave so that everyone could see who I was. But then the woman who had been in front of me in the line stood up and said, "How come he can say the n-word?" The bus driver looked back at me and said, "I didn't know you say that." I said, "I'm sorry. This is part of my Tourette syndrome. I can't help it."

She repeated herself: "Well, I didn't know you say that word." And I said again, "Ma'am, I'm sorry. I wish I could help it, but there's nothing I can do."

Then she said, and this is verbatim: "Either you put a cotton ball in your mouth or you get the hell off my bus."

She stalked off the bus. I began to sweat, thinking this really isn't good. I was pissing off or frightening every single person on a large, crowded bus. Everyone was looking at me – and my friends. I felt like I was putting them in danger.

I jumped up, got off the bus and followed the driver into her office. I think she was calling management or the human resources department within Greyhound or something, trying to figure out what to do with me. In between calls, she kept asking me, "Why don't you say, 'cracker'? What's wrong with you? You can only say 'nigger'? Why aren't you saying, 'cracker'?"

Back on the bus, the passengers had started getting hostile with my friends – confronting them, asking who I thought I was and stuff like that. My friends were defending me, even though the other passengers were beginning to call them names. It was not a good situation.

Pretty soon, the police showed up. First on the scene was this enormous white guy with white hair. He started asking in this really belligerent way what was going on. I began to explain. But then more cops kept coming – three, four, five. In the end, seven cops came. Of course, each new officer just added to the confusion. Each one wanted me to start from the beginning, and they all kept asking the same thing: "What is this disorder and why do you have to say the n-word? Why can't you say other words?"

I started stressing out, of course. And, since stress exacerbates Tourette's, I started ticcing even more, which made all the police officers even more belligerent. It was getting really hairy.

One of the cops kept asking if I was on medication. Where was my medication? I kept explaining that while, yes, some people with Tourette's do take medication, I had never found any that helped so I didn't take any. I kept trying to explain that, even if I did take medication, I couldn't just take a pill and my Tourette's would be gone.

None of them had the slightest idea what Tourette's is. All they did was make the situation worse. I had already been ticcing "nigger" over and over again, non-stop. Soon, my head was shaking, totally out of control.

At some point, one of the officers got combative and accused me of trying to take one of his weapons. I think he was trying to provoke me into something they could arrest me for. He kept saying something about how he had six deadly weapons in his belt and accusing me of trying to take one. They took my friend Jodie into a separate room and started interrogating her. Another friend began throwing up in a trash can because he was so stressed out. It was a nightmare.

By then it was noon. It was incredibly hot that day. There were fans, everywhere, whirring away, but everyone was sweaty and kind of losing it. I had been trying to explain myself for an hour or more, and there was only so much explaining that I could do. I started sobbing. It hurt so much to feel like I was being rejected as a person. Imagine everyone on a bus singling you out and saying, "YOU!!! We don't want you here!"

How could they not see that underneath the Tourette's, which was just this surface symptom, I was a completely regular, vulnerable person like any of them?

The ironic thing about the situation was that, of all the people there, the most sympathetic besides my friends was this one black officer. Here were these six white cops, all going crazy because they couldn't figure out what to do with me, and here I was, freaking out, ticcing "nigger" over and over again, and the only cop with any understanding happened to be black. It may have been because he was young, and these other guys were older. I don't really know. I just remember him saying, "Sorry, man, there's nothing I can do. These guys don't understand." It was nice to have this guy be sympathetic, even if it didn't exactly turn the tide.

Finally, after many deliberations, one of the Greyhound supervisors came and said, "You're not allowed back on the bus." It was official: I was not going to be getting back on the bus. My friends decided not to leave me stranded. The bus took off – with my bags on it. So we were all stranded in Indianapolis because of me.

That's about when the local news reporters showed up with their cameras. I had called my parents to tell them what was going on, and they had immediately called the media, thinking that, if there were some outside witnesses, I would be safe. Which was pretty funny. One minute, I was sitting there, talking with the cops, going round and round, down this downward spiral. Then, all of a sudden, the media showed up – and the police just scattered.

Luckily, someone from the camp happened to live in St. Louis. Somehow, someone got in contact with him, and I hitched a ride home with him. My friends were allowed to get on the next bus. I beat them back to St Louis and actually met them at the Greyhound station to welcome them.

When I got home, my parents and I sat down and watched the news together. There I was, on TV, shaking my head and making all these noises. On the one hand, if you didn't know anything about Tourette's, I probably looked like a freak. But if you did know anything about it, you would just see this kid who was trying to keep his cool in an incredibly tense situation, trying to explain what was going on.

When the news segment was over, my parents and I had this complex moment. The whole incident had been absolutely terrifying. That's why I remember it vividly, 10 years later, with tears in my eyes. We'd been living with my Tourette's for a dozen years already. The idea that it could kick up such a fuss that it would end up on TV seemed crazy. This was normal for us. It was something we lived with every hour, every car trip, every holiday, in every classroom, in every room of our house, every day of our lives. As the newscast ended, we paused for a moment and took comfort in the fact that whatever had happened, here we were, together, safe and sound. There was nothing else to say. All we could do was shrug: just another day for the Elliots!

The Greyhound incident had a huge impact on me. I had met strangers before who had reacted to me in ways that were uncomfortable (for themselves and for me). But this was really the first time I grasped the extent of the intolerance I would face outside my tiny bubble of friends and family in Clayton, Missouri, where nearly everyone understood me.

I had naively assumed that the larger world would be just as understanding, and that people knew all about Tourette's. I was right in a small way: People had *heard* about Tourette's – they'd seen it on TV somewhere. But in terms of how they dealt with it when they bumped up against it in real life, I couldn't have been more wrong. People do not "get" Tourette's.

After the Greyhound incident, I realized that it wasn't wrong for black people in Indianapolis to get upset because a white kid came up to them and started saying the n-word. But even if their outrage was understandable, and even if I felt horrible about it, it still didn't change the fact that I deserved to be understood and tolerated, too. So what was I supposed to do? I decided I needed to start raising public awareness in whatever way I could.

The first time I ever came close to speaking out publicly about my disorder was in 10th grade. I was in drama class, and it was one of those days when everyone was misbehaving. My teacher got fed up with us and screamed, "OK, fine! I quit! You guys teach the class!" To punish us, she made us go home and prepare speeches for the next day. We had one night to prepare to speak about any topic we wanted, and then, bam, we had to get up in front of the whole class and give a speech.

I remember the speech vividly. The lights were off, and a spotlight shone on me. I had been in plays before, but those had been group collaborations, and I was always in character. I had made announcements to my classes before, explaining that I had Tourette's. But it was never just me, speaking as myself, explaining Tourette's in depth.

I was absolutely terrified – sweating and shaking. But at the same time, I loved it. It was liberating. For the first time in my life, I felt like I had some control. I finally had *time* to say what it was that I had been trying to say for a long, long time.

All my life, I'd been reacting. I'd gotten myself into a million jams and embarrassing situations, just by being me, going about my life. And every time, I'd gone into emergency defense mode, talking fast, joking, mincing and wincing my way out of it. I had handed out my cards, offering nice little definitions of Tourette's, always being worried that I was scaring people or interrupting their day, their meal, their walk in the park. Every step of the way, I was basically apologizing for being me. But never once had it really been me, talking from my own point of view in a calm, comprehensive way, framing the conversation on my own terms.

Speaking before a group, holding the floor, I felt this incredible feeling of finally having a moment to take a breath. It was such a relief that I felt like crying! I started by asking my peers, my friends, for the first time in my life, "Do you guys have any idea what it's like being me?" It's like I finally had permission to tell people on my own terms, "You know what? All my life, I've been hiding. And this is what I've been hiding."

After the Greyhound incident, at the start of my junior year, I met with the debate coach at school and asked what I should do to get some practice doing public speaking. She let me speak to some of her English classes. I met with the president of the St. Louis Tourette syndrome chapter to see if the group had any need for an outreach speaker.

I found opportunities to speak locally to a few different elementary and high schools. A friend's mom who taught at a local community college asked me to come speak to an education class. Then, when I was a senior, I was asked to speak at the statewide student council convention, a gathering of some 500 high school kids who had served on their student governments. It felt like the big time. I drove an hour and a half to get there, sweating the whole way.

I spoke about the Greyhound incident and about advocating for oneself. It was scary, but I felt good about it afterward. It was helpful to engage with people who were curious. It seemed right to be able to address people about my conditions and educate them. After every speech, I felt like, "OK, that's 15 more people who will get it from now on!" "OK, 32 more understanding people in the world." And speeches kept coming my way, every few months.

From a very young age, I'd been inspired by the woman who, along with my parents, had literally given me life: Dr. Jesse Ternberg had been the amazing surgeon who intervened at the hospital on the night the other doctors were going to let me die. From very early on in childhood, I wanted to be a pediatric surgeon so I could follow in her footsteps.

When I was her patient, she was so kind and caring toward me. During my many, many surgeries and hospital stays, she always took time to visit my room and talk to me. She would explain in a very adult, respectful way what was going on with my body and praise me for being so strong. I was in awe of her. I wanted to be just like her: not just a doctor, but someone who helped other people like she had helped me. I couldn't imagine anything more powerful for a person to do with his or her life. She showed me that people truly can be heroes in this world.

In elementary school, whenever we had a project to do, I always chose things that had to do with the human body. We used to have this thing called the Great Body Shop, which were pamphlets about the human body with all kinds of pictures. As early as first or second grade, I knew about intestines and the digestive system. In high school, I focused on biology classes. I loved learning about the body. Despite all my challenges, my erratic-seeming behavior, my physical zigzags and setbacks, my life trajectory had in many ways been very cookie-cutter. I'd always known exactly where I was going in life: I was going to college, I was going to take the pre-med requirements, and then I was going to med school.

It might seem like a crazy dream. After all, how would I do surgery or something requiring a high degree of coordination if I had a condition that caused me to have physical spasms? It's not like I ignored reality, but I decided not to let it bug me or stop me. I'd gotten past all my other challenges, and I would get through this, as well. I had had a conversation with my brother Brian about my becoming a doctor. He asked me why, and I said that I wanted to save lives and help people. He pointed out that there were other jobs, like being a therapist or a teacher, that also helped people. There are actually plenty of jobs that help people. But for me, once I had decided to become a doctor, that was it. I never questioned the decision again.

While most of my fellow high school students were agonizing about where to go to college, I already knew my path. I'd taken early decision to Washington University in St. Louis. It had been ranked one of the top 15 colleges in the country. This helped make my decision, but I also understood that college would be a lot less stress (socially, financially and in terms of my challenges) if I stayed close to home. I already had a network of doctors in place, and I knew how to get around. I knew where all the bathrooms were in St. Louis! Minimizing all these difficulties would help me concentrate on my studies.

Before classes started, my family met with school officials and discussed the potential issues my attendance might entail. It seemed inappropriate to put me in a regular room with a roommate because I would be ticcing and distracting them all the time. The school decided to put me in a four-person suite, where each person had his own room.

It was a good idea, but the result was mixed. Having a private room meant no roommates. It was great for my comfort level, but I learned from my friends who were going off to schools and sharing rooms that having a roommate tends to force you out of your shell. Both you and the roommate tend to leave the room more often and meet more people. You meet your roommate's friends, and they meet yours.

Our four-person suite was kind of off in its own world, away from the mainstream of freshman life. About half the people on my floor were sophomores, so I never got that rowdy, freshman experience where everyone parties and hangs out and gets to meet each other. I kept seeing students in the other dorms having these amazing experiences. I wasn't having anything like that.

During the first week of school, I was using one of the computers in the student union. The girl next to me – who happened to be super cute – kept looking at me. Of course, this made me nervous, so I started ticcing even more loudly and frequently than usual. She finally gave me this incredibly mean look, and honestly, it looked like she was snarling as she said, "God! You are so f......g annoying."

I began to go into my people-pleasing routine, which I by then realized I needed to do every time I entered a new social environment. I would ingratiate myself with people and show them that I was funny and normal, apart from my tics. I was getting pretty good at it. But my relationships felt desperate and superficial. I was making new friends. They just didn't feel as fun or close as my old friends. I wasn't creating that bond I'd gotten used to.

There was a café inside the campus library called Whispers. I spent a lot of time there studying. The walls were made entirely out of glass. The café was still part of the library, so you were supposed to be quiet. It made for a strange scene: me, sitting in a café called Whispers, ticcing and barking and doing my thing while people peered at me through the glass.

I hate to admit this, but I started to get insecure and mopey.

I had always done well in school, but I'd never had to compete like this. There were 1,400 kids studying in my class at Washington U, and 600 of them were pre-med. In the end, three-quarters of the pre-med students either changed majors or dropped out. There was a heavy-duty weeding-out process from the very beginning. I don't know if I wasn't ready for it or I was depressed, but in my first semester chemistry class, I got a C. I'd never gotten a C before.

And despite my efforts to make friends and be "fun" around people, I still felt isolated. Over winter break, I went on a group trip to Israel. At a pit stop somewhere, I went into a bathroom. I was in there, pooping, when a group of army guys entered. They noticed my noises and started commenting and laughing. This group of really macho dudes in their army fatigues, carrying machine guns, were standing outside my stall, listening to me, laughing hysterically. It was humiliating.

Around that time, I went out to a club one night with a group of new friends. There was a girl with us. I thought she was the most gorgeous girl on campus. We went out dancing and, at some point during the evening, we ended up making out. I was so excited. It was like a dream come true to be making out with this girl. I was still a virgin, and I was thinking, "Oh boy! Tonight's the night! It's gonna happen! It's finally gonna happen!" The entire night, my mind was racing.

We had all driven in my car so when we got back to campus, I dropped everyone off, one by one, including the girl, who had invited me back to her place. Instead of just parking, which would have only taken a couple minutes, I realized that I had better go to the bathroom, too. After all, since we were likely going to be getting extremely intimate, I wouldn't want to interrupt the proceedings to go take a big, noisy poop that would surely freak her out. I raced back home, and I guess I was kind of stressed out. I was trying so hard to poop it took me 25 minutes. By the time I finally got to her dorm, she was lying lethargically on her bed. She gave me this look like, "Oh yeah, you." And then she said, "Yeah, umm, I think I'm gonna crash."

I can't say the episode did wonders for my self-esteem, but it was the kind of thing that characterized my first semester of college.

Throughout college, I continued to give presentations here and there about Tourette's. I spoke about a lot of different topics, like overcoming obstacles, loving yourself and advocating for yourself, but my main focus was trying to get people to understand me. I handed out index cards to members of the audience, each with a number and a different tic on it. Number 4 might say, "Bark like a dog." Number 7 might say, "Chomp your teeth." At random moments, I'd hold up one of the index cards with a number, and, if the audience was playing along, whoever had card 4 would bark like a dog, and whoever had 7 would chomp his or her teeth. It was great. It made people laugh, but it also helped them identify with what it would be like to have Tourette's.

As I got more practice, I realized that public speaking affected me in a very profound way. It allowed me to be honest in a way that I couldn't be in my regular life. In real life, with most of my new schoolmates, I couldn't let down my guard. When I gave a speech, even though I was talking to a group of strangers, I had to fill up the time. I had to say something interesting, and the truth was always the most interesting thing to say. I would tell people about my poops, about my offensive speech – everything.

I began to realize the power of being honest. As I learned how to be honest about myself, I began painting a fuller picture of how my disorders had affected me. I was learning as much from my speeches as anyone in the audience was!

I spoke at a conference for people with Tourette's, and I met a kid there who was talking about how he suppresses his tics when he's at school. It drove me nuts to think about it. I'd spent my whole eighth grade trying to suppress my tics, waiting until I came home to unleash all of my crazy energy. And it hurt me. Physically and emotionally, it was one of the most painful things I'd ever experienced. It made me upset to think anyone else should ever try to do this. When you're suppressing a tic, all you can think is, "Oh my God. Oh my God, this hurts so bad." All your energy goes into *not* doing something. It's exhausting, mentally and emotionally, and it limits you from accomplishing things with whatever talents you have.

By not suppressing, you free yourself from the pain, but you also gain a life: You free your mind to focus on things like learning, listening, caring about other people, observing the world beyond you.

My question to the kid was, "Isn't this incredibly uncomfortable? Why would you do this?" You didn't cause this disorder!" The questions weren't only for the boy; they applied to me, too. How much was I still suppressing?

I thought about the example my parents set for me – by advocating for me, by making sure challenges never shut me down. I thought about how they had pushed me. I thought about how they had worked to get me to summer camp. About how they printed out cards, explaining my disorder, so that situations were more comfortable for me and the people around me. They taught me the invaluable lesson of making elbow room for myself in the world.

But in the end, no one would teach me more about advocacy than my brother Brian. To tell the full story, I have to take a break from my own and go back in time. When I was in sixth grade and he was in 10th, Brian came out of the closet. He told us – and the world – who he really was. Brian is gay.

Ever since he was a kid, Brian had known he was different. As far back as kindergarten, he remembered chasing some boy around, trying to kiss him. When he was in first grade, he had a crush on two identical twin boys. At the same time, he found it more natural to socialize with girls; he preferred hopscotch over kickball, jump-rope over football, choir over soccer.

He eventually figured out what was going on. This was before there were many positive gay role models in the media, before Ellen DeGeneres, before Will & Grace. Now, it's not uncommon to see gay politicians, gay business executives, gay leaders in many different careers, but back then, the only gay people Brian could take stock of were typically hairdressers or fashionistas. He didn't identify with any of them.

Surely, he thought, life hadn't intended for him to end up this way. Being gay meant he could never get married or have a family. He could never serve in the military. Gay people weren't protected by hate crime or employment laws, at least, not in Missouri.

He couldn't imagine what he had had done to deserve what he thought was such an abominable orientation. Whenever he heard people discussing homosexuality as a personal choice, it made him cringe. Why would he be so stupid as to choose a sexual orientation that would be so unaccepted and painful?

It's interesting, in some ways, to note the parallels between Brian and me. Both of us were "cursed," or so it seemed to us, with a condition we hadn't chosen that got more and more difficult with time.

As Brian entered junior high school, he became more fearful. Keeping his secret became stressful. It was a dark and lonely period. Some of his meaner peers jeered him for being a "sissy." He acquired what he called "the golden boy complex." The more he feared his secret would be discovered, the more adamantly he set out to prove to the world how perfect he was.

When he was in sixth grade, he started a carnival in our back yard and donated all the proceeds to Children's Hospital, where I had spent so many months of my life. In seventh grade, he started something called the Achievement Forest, a program to recognize kids for their inner qualities, not just for their grades or outer achievements. Each year, 50 students got a tree to plant around the middle school. (Twenty years later, the trees have formed a forest around our old school!) He later started something called Deaf Link, which connected high school students with kids who are deaf. *Teen People* magazine wrote a story about him for that.

No question about it, my brother was the golden boy – on the outside. On the inside, he hated himself. When he was 13, he bought some books on hypnosis. He tried the experiments they suggested. Nothing. He tried borrowing *Playboy* magazines from his friends and masturbating to them. Maybe, he thought, he could force the issue and corral his body chemistry toward heterosexuality. Of course, it didn't work. After a while, he became one of those LGBT (Lesbian, Gay, Bisexual and Transgender) kids who consider suicide because they can't imagine the repercussions of living authentic lives. It was understandable for him to feel that way. Again, there was a parallel between him and me because I knew all too well that Missouri wasn't the most tolerant place for people with differences. Like me, Brian tried incredibly hard to please people. And, like me, it never seemed to work. It never seemed to be enough.

He daydreamed about taking his own life. He even settled on the perfect way: He'd sit in the car, in the garage, with the car running. For months, the plan turned itself over and over in his head. But the thought of hurting my parents kept him from taking any actual steps to end his life.

One day, he found a gay and lesbian chat room on America Online and hit upon a brilliant plan. He'd invented the perfect lie. He started doing research and trying to engage the older lesbians online to help him with his plan. Would one of them ever be interested in marrying him, when he was a bit older? He and the lesbian could marry and move next door to a house occupied by Brian's *real* spouse and the lesbian's *real* partner – who, of course, would also be legally married to each other. Behind the acceptable, traditional façade, the two men could live in one house, the two women could live in the other, and everyone would be happy. Whenever parents and co-workers came over for dinner, the "spouses" could switch places and make home life look normal! At 13, Brian saw this convoluted plan as his ticket to finding acceptance publicly and finding love privately.

The plan fell apart pretty quickly. As it turned out, there just weren't a whole lot of older lesbians interested in discussing marriage with a 13-year-old boy. Hmm.

My brother finally had a spiritual epiphany when he was 16. It was 1997. He'd gone on a youth trip to Israel. One evening, high on a mountain, watching the sun set over a beautiful Egyptian skyline, he felt himself having a sort of conversation with God. Basically, he was pissed off. He asked God, "Look, if You exist, why would You both make me the way I am and then say in the Bible, 'You shouldn't be gay'?" To him, this sure seemed like an awful loophole or a terrible oversight. Why would God make someone a certain way if it is forbidden and reviled? The same Bible says we're all created in God's image.

Unlike Moses, Brian didn't get a parchment note or a stone tablet from God, telling him what to do. But he did experience a breakthrough: There is no valor in going through life living a lie. God had surely not intended for him to live a miserable life and make everyone else around him miserable, too. It was time to speak up and surrender to honesty. If society wanted to make his life miserable, fine. But no more would he continue torturing himself by being dishonest. He wanted to live a life full of love and happiness, just like everyone else. He even wanted a family someday. For the first time in his life, he believed he could have all of those things.

He walked back down the mountain and began to spit out the truth to his friends. It took him half an hour to get the words out. But he did it. And, for the first time in his life, he felt free. It was exhilarating.

Ten days later, Brian returned home and told our parents and his closest friends. No more secrets. Done.

I remember distinctly how I experienced all of this. I was sitting on the couch, watching TV. Suddenly, my mom looked in and asked me to come into the kitchen. I knew something was wrong. Her tone was off. She sounded tense. I entered the kitchen as cautiously as I could, suspecting trouble of some kind.

There was a dim light over the kitchen table, almost like one of those bare bulbs hanging over a table in an interrogation scene in a movie. The silence was buzzing in my ear. Everything was flashing through my mind. Were my parents going to have another baby? Had someone died? I sat down and sank into my chair. Only then did I realize my dad was in the room, too. I hadn't seen him. Obviously, whatever was about to unfold was *serious*.

The conversation started with my mom talking about how sometimes people are different. Different in their race, color, ethnicity and even sexual preferences. My dad joined in and helped her finish her sentences. Sometimes, they continued, people have to deal with difficult issues. But whatever these issues are, they don't change who we are. Because we're ultimately all the same. We're all human.

Then they both just blurted out, "Brian is gay."

I was about to ask if they were kidding, but then I saw that my mom was crying and my dad's eyes were filling up with buckets of water. Then I was crying, too. I just froze. "My big brother is gay," I thought. "My brother is gay."

What did that mean? I thought of stereotype gays on TV, getting their nails done, talking in what seemed to be fake, high-pitched voices. Like Brian, I had never met an openly gay person before, or at least never knew that I had. Was my brother going to change and become like the gay people on TV? Why had I been so oblivious to this? How could I not have known he was gay? The absence of girlfriends, the prevalence of female friends – these suddenly seemed like obvious clues.

But the more I thought about it, the more I realized how un-obvious it really was. Brian wasn't swishy or flamboyant. He wasn't fixated on fashion and hairstyles. He didn't look like any of the gay stereotypes I'd seen. He was the antithesis of my stereotypical perception of gays.

I was still processing this when I heard footsteps coming down the stairs. Brian appeared in the doorway, looking exactly the same as he'd ever looked. "Hey, Marc," he smiled. I stood up and the rest was pretty automatic. He was still my brother. Nothing else mattered. I gave him a big hug that seemed to last for an eternity. From that point on, our family had changed.

News of my brother's coming out traveled fast in suburban St. Louis. My brother was well-known and well-regarded at school and in the broader community. For many in our community, he was the first "out" gay person they had ever known. Most of our family and friends were shocked to hear the news.

But as Brian continued his coming-out process, his courage and his character made people question the very stereotypes that even I once believed. Here he was an intelligent and motivated student, a student government representative, the founder of several community-service programs, a popular and well-liked kid. He didn't fit the profile of what people thought it meant to be LGBT. He began to feel his own power to change people's attitudes.

Brian became an advocate about gay issues. He began by speaking at his high school. The principal let him address the whole school to tell his story and ask for acceptance. It was pretty amazing. After high school, he joined what was called the superintendent's advisory board, and he helped persuade the school district to stop discriminating against gay teachers and include protection for gay students in the anti-bullying policy. In college, he joined a student speakers bureau, going around to college dorms, sharing his story, answering questions about gay life and dispelling harmful myths people had believed their entire lives. At Harvard Business School, he went on to become the co-president of the LGBT student association.

My brother has gone on to become an ever-more forceful advocate for gay freedoms. His full-time job is a nonprofit organization he founded called Friendfactor, which is devoted to fighting for equal rights for LGBT Americans and ending the employment, marital and housing prejudices that single out gays for separate treatment under the law. He has become a model for success and inspiration to me and many thousands of others by standing up for what he believes.

Of course, at the time my brother was going through his journey, from closeted gay teen to confident adult activist, I was still a kid. It had to be painful for him to be around me. He had gone off to college and was doing a lot of his own public speaking, talking to students about tolerance. Then he'd come home on vacation, and all I could do was tic: "You're gay!" And "Faggot!" "Faggot!" "Faggot!" It was the worst name I could call him, and yet I did so thousands and thousands of times.

He must have wanted to kill me even though he knew I couldn't stop myself. In the end, his message and his activism would have a huge effect on me and my understanding of the world.

As I got older, I realized how much courage he had shown in standing up for himself. I couldn't yet live up to his example. It would take many years before I could. But he definitely turned on a light and showed me a way that I would later strive to follow.

By transforming himself from a shy, closeted, depressed and suicidal teen to a confident adult leader, I had watched him transform his biggest (perceived) liability into his greatest source of strength. Was there anything I might be able to learn from his story? Time would tell.

A t the end of first semester, I won a small scholarship from one of the fraternities at Washington U. Through the process of accepting the award, I met some fraternity members. I had never, ever thought much about fraternities, and I had definitely never imagined myself joining one. Before college, my perception of fraternities was based on the movie "Animal House": people drinking all the time and being crazy, hazing recruits in sadistic ways and vomiting a lot. It didn't seem like my cup of tea. But after meeting some "fraternity brothers" who seemed like regular human beings, I thought, "Hey, they're not so bad. In fact, these guys are pretty cool."

When second semester began, rush week came. That's where you go around to different activities and outings on campus and check out the different frats. Although I hadn't quite expected it, one of them, which I'll call Alpha Beta, gave me a bid, which is like an invitation to pledge.

The pledging period lasts for three months. And what it consists of, as with all fraternities, is basically undergoing a series of tests and mild humiliations. The point of their tricks and rituals was not to make us suffer, but to bring the fellow pledges closer together. When the other pledges and I got our bids, we were told to report at a specific time to the fraternity's off-campus housing, wearing a suit. Each of us arrived, dressed in a suit, none of us knowing each other in the slightest. We were standing there, waiting, when suddenly, three upperclassmen from the fraternity broke into the room shouting and swearing at us. It was so dramatic. It was exhilarating. They started yelling at me because I hadn't shaved. "It's supposed to be formal attire!! What's wrong with you??" Another shouted: "This is the ugliest pledge class I've seen in 20 years!" They ordered us to march across campus to the fraternity.

Once there, they gave us a CD with a song to memorize. Then they made us all go over to a small room in the house. They turned out the lights and shut the door, warning us that we had to be absolutely silent – or else. We were supposed to just stand there – for two hours. It was kind of agonizing. Of course, before long, I started ticcing. "I have to poop dad!!" I kept saying. Before long, we were cracking up.

Pledging for this house was incredibly mild. The upperclassmen were supposed to intimidate us and be sadistic, but these guys were very bad sadists! When we were in the room, just standing there, and I started ticcing, one of the older brothers came over to me and whispered gently, "Look, if you really have to go, you don't have to do this."

The brother in charge of getting us through the initiation rites was known as the pledge master. His whole job was to be rock-solid mean. He was supposed to be our enemy, more or less responsible for our humiliation. But even he couldn't keep it up.

One time, the pledges and I were gathered outside the fraternity house. We had all been assigned a number, from 1 to 22, and whenever we were told to come to the house, we had to wait outside in total silence for the entire group to assemble. When the pledge master arrived, we were supposed to count off. If someone was missing or if we messed up the count, we had to start all over again. Even after the count was finished, we were to remain silent as we awaited further instructions. So, of course, I couldn't help it; I start ticcing. "rectum!!! rectum!" The pledge master burst out laughing. He couldn't help it. Everyone else burst out laughing, too.

The brothers I met were great. They knew about my challenges, but they didn't seem to care that much. I was different from anyone they'd ever met, but they neither treated me like a freak nor were they overly cautious around me. They hadn't chosen me because I was a weirdo; they just seemed genuinely to feel like I'd make a good addition to the group. In a lot of ways, the pledge period was like high school: a mix of fun, agony and weirdness. Many of the fraternity brothers ended up becoming my best friends. But I couldn't help always wondering in the back of my mind, unconsciously: "When is this going to get easier?"

My health issues kept throwing me surprises. During pledge time, I went out to dinner with my friend and his dad, who was a doctor. As we were eating, the doctor looked at me and said, "Kid, you look anemic."

I went to the hospital for what I thought would be a routine blood test. By the time I had gotten home, hospital staff had called and told me to get back to the hospital – immediately. Apparently, I'd been bleeding from my rectum – a lot – due to all the wear and tear on it from my weird method of pooping and from all the surgeries I'd had over the years. I'd often noticed bleeding, but I'd always ignored it. It turned out that my iron level was ridiculously low from all the blood I'd lost.

They put me on a three-month program. Each week, I went to the hospital for an iron infusion and a visit with Linda the Rectal Therapist. Yes, you read that correctly, Linda the Rectal Therapist.

I would go to her office, which was part of a physical therapy clinic. I'd walk in, and there'd be a half-dozen patients sitting in the lobby. We'd sit and watch patients working out in a kind of gym, with the help of a handful of other physical therapists. Everyone would be wearing sweats and gym clothes except me, the college kid. Linda would come out in her white lab coat to get me. All the patients and physical therapists would watch her lead me out of the lobby. They knew what was going to happen. Every time, I felt like I was walking the plank.

Linda's office was tiny. We'd enter, she'd leave, and I would get naked except for my shirt. I'd put this little cloth thing around my waist, which was kind of a joke because it was so tiny, and then I'd sit down on the examination table.

Linda would enter and take a seat next to me. I'd turn on my side, with my knees up near my chest. She'd place electrodes around my rectum. She had a very kind, pleasant, teacher-y, maternal kind of face, and she tried her best to make small talk. I tried my best to act like this was no big deal, that I had conversations all the time while people were fiddling around with my rectum.

"So, Marc, how's school going? How are your classes?"

"Oh, um, (gulp), It's um, O-OK."

"Yeah, you're enjoying school? That's great!"

At that point, she'd roll me over on the other side and have me look at a computer screen. It was exactly like when I was in 10th grade and the neuro-feedback doctor tested my brain. My butt-hole was connected by wires to a computer, and the basic idea was that I would learn to control my muscles by seeing what my body did.

In short, Linda was trying to re-train me how to poop in a less harmful way. When most people poop, they don't do it by squeezing; they do it by relaxing their butt muscles. It's much more about letting go than it is about force. When I pooped, however, I was forcing it out, again and again. That's what was causing me harm. Linda's computer was supposed to help show me when I was relaxed, and when I wasn't, so I could learn by seeing.

When my anus muscles were tight, the lines on the graph would go up. When I relaxed, the muscles would go down. Linda would sit there talking to me, getting me to squeeze my butt-hole muscles and then relax them, watching the graph go up and down.

Squeeze. Relax. Squeeze. Relax.

Then Linda would put her finger up my butt hole and then say, "Relax now!" She could tell if I was relaxing the right way or not.

Finally, she would grab two paper towels and say, "OK! I'm going to wipe you now." Then she'd wipe my butt. I was 19 years old and a grown woman was wiping my ass.

Then I would go to the bathroom, poop, change back into my clothes. For the finale, she would tell me some more exercises I needed to work on before I returned. I would walk out, past all the senior citizens in the physical therapy room. I'd go back to college and see my fellow students, doing their thing. It seemed surreal. Here I was in college, where most kids were having sex, smoking pot and studying. Instead, I was meeting on the sly with Linda the Rectal Therapist.

I lived in the frat house for my sophomore year and first semester of my junior year. For the second semester of junior year, I went to London for a study abroad program. After getting the C in first semester chemistry class, I rallied. My GPA was not perfect, but good: 3.4. My sophomore year, I was elected to a prestigious student club called Lock and Chain, which only invited 15 students to join. I'd been both rush chair and philanthropy chair at the fraternity. Having the brothers welcome me in had been a game-changer. It really improved my happiness.

When I first moved into the house, I had a single room. But I had to share a bathroom with three other guys. There was a stall door for the toilet, a sink and a shower, which meant that it happened quite often that multiple people were in the bathroom at the same time. It was the first time I'd ever had to share a bathroom outside my family and the first time I'd had to live in such close quarters with strangers. It was intense, way outside of my comfort zone.

At the beginning, I warned everyone around me every time I was going to the bathroom. If someone was already in the bathroom, showering, I would ask, "Hey, is it OK if I poop?" It goes without saying that my retraining sessions with Linda hadn't helped me any more than the sessions with the neuro-biologist in eighth grade had helped me learn to be less stressed out. I learned the correct way to go to the bathroom but found it incredibly difficult to change the way I did it, day to day. My habits were so ingrained.

My new living situation at the house was tense. It really was. No one ever told me whether I was bugging them or grossing them out, so I never knew. I would do everything possible to be quiet. I would try to minimize the number of times I sucked air in and out of myself, and it was not easy. It was excruciating, actually. When I finally did let Mother Nature fly, I felt nauseated with self-disgust. Inside, I'd be boiling with shame. My mind would be screaming: "You're so loud! This is disgusting!! You're disgusting!"

Our memories are so fickle. Until I sat down to write this, I had completely forgotten how painful this was. I remember this part of my life as being an incredible time. But when I break down the moments, it's almost schizophrenic. On the one hand, I was really loving my life, loving the frat, loving my new friends. At the same time, every time I took a dump, I was undergoing severe panic that I would be rejected.

The first few times I went to the bathroom, I walked out of the stall terrified. No one ever gave me a hard time about it. One guy gave me a couple of looks but never said anything.

Sometimes there were girls visiting, hanging out with guys. Whatever worries I had around my housemates would, of course, become 10 times bigger. There was one secluded bathroom on an upper floor, which I could occasionally sneak into without getting caught. It was weird to be living in a house, a fraternity, a brotherhood, but also be simultaneously tip-toeing around, stealthily searching out some place to poop where no one could hear me!

"Marc, you know, we wanted to have you on the team, but basically, people just didn't know."

People just didn't know. People just didn't know what?

During my freshman year, I had heard about a student-run EMT service on campus. It was like a junior ambulance corps. I thought it would be perfect experience for a guy who wanted to get into med school. I was totally qualified: I was physically fit, my résumé was stellar, I had written a good application essay, and I knew a lot of the other students who were working there.

But, even though I made it through the entire interview process flawlessly, they rejected me. I was stunned. Why? I was every bit as qualified as the other candidates who'd been accepted. In fact, I found out later that I had correctly answered some trick questions they'd given – which other applicants had failed. Yet they had chosen those other applicants to be on the team and not me.

I later met up with one of the people involved in the decision. And that's when he confessed: "Marc, you know, we wanted to have you on the team, but basically, people just didn't know." I can never forget those words, even today. What he meant was that they didn't know, for example, what might happen if we came across a black patient and I started ticcing. It was horrible. I knew that my disorder wouldn't affect my ability to care for someone's health. I thought it was unfair that they were making assumptions about my limitations. It was the first big danger sign I got about my career path.

I had known from a very young age that I wanted to be a doctor, but I had almost never questioned whether my medical issues would hinder me from getting there. The few times I did pause to question, the answer I got back from everyone, and from the universe itself, had always seemed to be: "YES, MARC. BE A DOCTOR!" Now I had to ask myself, if my main objective was simply to serve others, weren't there other occupations that I could choose? Why did I absolutely have to be a doctor?

I spent the summer after sophomore year studying for the Medical College Admission Test (MCAT). The MCAT is more or less the equivalent to the SAT or ACT tests for college, except it's for medical school. Most people take the MCAT at the end of their junior year, but I was hoping to go abroad for the second semester. This meant rushing all my pre-med classes and cramming everything in early to take the test before I headed abroad. I was eager to get this hurdle to my life plans out of the way.

When I had taken the ACT in high school, a counselor helped me arrange to take the test in a private room so my tics wouldn't distract others. Secondly, test administrators gave me time-and-a-half for the test to make up for the time I lost from my tics. I figured I would ask for the same kind of buffer for the MCAT. After all, this was probably the most important test I would be taking in my entire life.

The MCAT administrators surprised me. They took forever to write back, and, when they did, they agreed to grant me a private room but argued that I hadn't provided enough documentation to show that I needed extra time for the test. I sent a letter from my neurologist, arguing my case, but it didn't convince them. I got into this endless battle with them, full of red tape. It went on for a year and a half. I kept postponing taking the MCAT because I assumed that I would eventually come to an agreement with the MCAT board. The matter was still unresolved when I went abroad second semester of junior year.

In the end, I lost. For once, my efforts to advocate for myself didn't win the day. I finally accepted that I just had to take the test and see how I'd do. In August 2007, right before senior year started, I took the test. The board followed through on getting me a private room, but I was really nervous. I wasted a lot of time ticcing and stressing, then stressing out about the time I was wasting by ticcing, then ticcing more from the stress, then stressing more from the tics, and so on.

I knew even as I finished the test that I had done poorly. And I was right. The maximum score you can get on the MCAT is a 45. No one gets that, but you really need a 30 to get into a decent med school. I did great on the science sections of the test, but my verbal scores were awful. I got a 28. I knew I could have scored higher if I'd had more time to make up for the time I had spent ticcing.

This was the first time I ever felt like my disability was going to ruin my career plans. Maybe I had gotten arrogant. All my life, I had faced and overcome one struggle after another. Not this time.

I was completely depressed.

Somewhere during the long fight with the MCAT board, I decided to take a year off after graduation. A lot of my friends had decided to do the same thing. We knew that going from high school to college to med school to residencies of three to seven years and then directly into professional life without a break was a recipe for a horrible life. We thought it seemed like a good time to take a break, travel abroad, do volunteer jobs, whatever might make life more interesting before getting on the career treadmill.

I would spend part of my year off studying for a second attempt at the MCAT. I knew this test was crucial for getting into a good school, and I didn't want it to derail my plans. But, at the same time, I hit upon an idea that seemed to come from way out of left field. Instead of working at a hospital during my year off, which is what most med students do (because it looks good on a med school application), I decided to go on a speaking tour. Never mind that I had never spoken outside the St. Louis area. Never mind that I had been paid for it only once – $200. Never mind that I didn't know how to get speaking jobs and didn't really have any idea about how to speak professionally.

I thought of all the volunteer speeches I had done: What if I could turn them into something more legitimate? I thought that even with a bad MCAT score, if I could pull off an impressive "speaking tour" around the country, it would completely negate my shortcomings, everything would be OK, and I'd get into a decent school.

First semester of senior year, I started taking special practice tests that simulated the actual MCAT. Over and over, drill after drill. Every time I did it, I found that, if I gave myself extra time, like I had requested, I got decent scores. Whenever I took a practice test in the normal amount of time allotted, I kept getting the same low score I got when I took the test for real. So, while I kept fighting the MCAT board for more time, I also kept trying to get so good at the test that I could raise my score even without it.

During this time, I kept thinking about content for my so-far imaginary speaking tour. It was one thing to tell people, "Oh, yeah. I'm taking a year off before medical school to go around the country and do a speaking tour." But *what*, exactly, was I going to be offering people? I didn't know. As I looked back on my life, through all the challenges, through all the obstacles, the bus story, the poops, what could be the most authentic, genuine, helpful topic I could speak about? Up until this point, whenever I'd had to speak, I had merely discussed a lot of random stuff. If someone came up to me and asked, "Marc, what do you speak about it?" I couldn't say. Or if I tried to say, I would have given different answers. I talked about overcoming challenges. I talked about advocacy. I talked about tolerance. I needed something more focused. Something strong.

What had I been doing this past seven years? I'd been trying to get people to understand me and tolerate me. So I made a decision that my speaking would be about tolerance. The first title I came up with for my speech was "Don't Judge a Book by Its Noises." This was a play on noises from both my ends! Funny. Right? OK, maybe not. But I thought so.

I put together a marketing package for my imaginary speaking tour. My friend Jodie's father ran a printing company, and with his help, I put together clippings about my previous speaking engagements and some letters of recommendation from people who had hired me for gigs. It took a long time to do it in a semi-professional way because I'd never done anything like this before. The more I thought about it, the more invested I got. I was excited: The idea of going around the country, speaking before audiences, seemed fun, challenging – exciting.

In March, the MCAT board had made a final decision. It would not allow me extra time. I wasn't completely surprised, but it wasn't the best news I could have heard. I didn't think, "Oh, this is a death sentence." I just thought, "Wow, you're *really* going to have to work hard. This is going to be severe."

When graduation came, in May, I still felt daunted by the test before me. Not many of my friends had applied to schools yet, so at least I wasn't hanging out with a bunch of smug people who would soon be running off to Harvard Medical School. But everyone around me had done well enough on the test not to have to spend weeks and weeks preparing to retake the MCAT. They were moving on. For them, graduation was party time. I wasn't feeling it.

There was only one bright spot for me: A few weeks earlier, I had been looking through the school newspaper and saw a picture of Dr. T. She had been selected to receive an honorary degree at my graduation. It was huge. I couldn't help but feel that this was some kind of serendipitous moment.

Graduation was a very emotional experience for me. I remember it so well: The sun was beating down. The speakers were reverberating throughout the quad. Fifteen thousand people were gathered outside, before the stage. When they called Dr. T to the stage to receive her degree, I was riveted. Here was the doctor who saved my life. Fifteen thousand people were watching her. They were all watching the person and admiring this stranger, who had done something honorable, but for me, her honor was personal: I owed my existence to her.

Ironically, the only reason she had been admitted to medical school was that when she applied, the people reviewing the applications thought "Jesse Ternberg" was a man. Once they let her in by mistake, they had to let her stay. She was the first woman to graduate from her class. Had this woman not had the courage to be a pioneer and a fighter, I would not be alive.

And there I was, sitting in my seat, following a path to be just like her. I looked down at my hands and couldn't hold back the tears. I turned to my friend, Andy: "Can you believe the power of one doctor?" I asked. "She's why I'm here."

It completely rejuvenated my commitment to become a doctor. It was so obvious: This was my calling. It was inevitable. With medical issues like mine, I would be the most sympathetic, excellent doctor the world had ever known.

O ver the summer, I continued studying. I was still depressed. I had no job and only one speaking gig that summer. I was very unhappy about a relationship. Well, it wasn't a relationship anymore; the relationship had ended, but my obsession about it was still going strong. And that was before I found out she was dating a fraternity brother of mine. Her name was Elsa, and all day long I kept thinking about her. And him. And her. And him. Minus me, the loser.

It was particularly painful because Elsa was the first woman I'd ever had a real relationship with. The end of it had made me consider my long, painful history of relationships.

I hadn't always been so hopeless. When I was a kid, I was completely girl-crazy. I had my first kiss on the lips in third grade – Annie Berk, underwater, in a pool. It was very steamy.

In seventh grade I had a girlfriend – Sarah Penn – for about 10 seconds.

In ninth grade, there was Margot Singer. We definitely went at it hot and heavy – for a minute, anyway.

Up until about ninth grade, I had been a total horndog. Even with my Hirschsprung's, I could overcome a lot of my fears when girls were involved. But, as we got into middle school and my Tourette's worsened, everything started to get scary. On top of that was puberty. Girls started getting boobs. Me and the other guys started to get horny – or in my case, hornier. Our bodies were changing, and the tensions kind of raised. Basically, all my fears started getting much bigger. And that made my Tourette's get even worse. Which then made me even more self-conscious around girls. I suddenly started to get much shyer. Things began to get much more complicated when it came to intimacy.

In 10th grade, I had my first real girlfriend – Mindy. The night of our homecoming dance, Mindy and I went out to dinner and had an amazing meal. We got to school for the dance at about eight o'clock.

Around nine o'clock we were out on the dance floor, having a great time. Then, all of a sudden, I got a red flag that said, "Uh-oh. Time to go to the bathroom."

Mindy knew I had Tourette's. I couldn't hide that. She had a little mole on her back, and I would tic "mole' every time I was with her. And other girls' names. And bad words, and all the other things I ticced all the time.

She knew about my Hirschsprung's, but she had no idea about my liquid poops, the frequency of them, the noise, or any of that. Back in 10th grade, almost nobody knew about that side of me.

I was about to freak out and panic, and all I could manage was to blurt out the words, "Mindy, I gotta go." I just left her on the dance floor. I was too embarrassed to tell her I was going to the bathroom because, even though that normally would not be a big thing for someone to say, in my mind, going to the bathroom was a huge, huge, huge thing. I couldn't talk about it. I didn't know how. So I just left her there.

At my school, they had given me permission to use a special restroom. I even had my own set of keys. But after leaving the auditorium, where the dancing was taking place, I realized that I hadn't driven that night. We had rented a limo for the evening. It had seemed like a very cool, suave, adult idea. Except now I realized I didn't have my car keys, which also meant I didn't have the special bathroom keys!

I began to run-walk like crazy, trying to seem calm, looking for the principal, until finally I found him. Every step of the way, I was positive I was going to dump in my pants – which would definitely have put a damper on things between Mindy and me.

Finally, I found the principal. He understood that I was in a hurry, that I was panicking, and he gave me his own personal set of keys for his private bathroom. Very trusting. No questions asked. Cool.

But then I faced a huge issue: How was I supposed to get to the principal's office without anyone seeing me? To get there, you had to walk up a staircase that was in plain sight of everyone on the dance floor. If Mindy had seen me, she probably would have come to the conclusion that I was ditching her – or doing something I shouldn't be.

My little brother, Justin, used to recite this funny thing when he was a kid. It was a list of things I would never be able to do because of my Tourette's. He was only nine at the time, but he'd say, "Marc: first, you can never be the winner of a game of hide-and-go-seek. Two, you can never be a librarian. Three, you can't be a robber. And four, you'll never be an operational command officer that goes on silent operation missions."

I thought of him at that moment because I was about to prove him wrong. There I was, wearing a suit and tie, on a secret mission to take a big, long, noisy poop and not get caught by my date. As I slithered and crab-walked and crouched my way up the stairs, hiding behind the little partition wall, waist-high. An alarming thought kept looping through my head. "What will people think if they see me?" I could just imagine the questions: "Dude! What are you doing?"

Finally, I made it. Mission accomplished. I crapped. And I didn't do it in my pants. I returned to the dance floor and resumed my date with Mindy. And yet. Mindy's and my relationship didn't last long after that – maybe a few weeks more. We got through the homecoming dance OK, but of course, she had wondered why I "ditched her" for 20 minutes during the dance. It was understandable that she was upset, but I could never explain. I just didn't know how to talk about it.

This was the beginning of me not really being able to be there for a relationship, and it was the beginning of me becoming extremely paranoid about my body. It was the beginning of me, Mr. Openness, keeping a lot to myself. Tenth and 11th grades were by far my worst years with the Tourette's and the OCD, and that was definitely a huge part of it. But I became terrified at the thought of intimacy. What would happen if I was going at it with a girl, and I pooped a little bit? What if she was touching me, and she touched poop? What if I left some on her bed? What if she smelled something? Everything connected to relationships during this period was difficult.

There was one girl I kissed. Mid-kiss, I started ticcing her mom's name. Talk about awkward.

This kind of thought filled every moment of intimacy with pure fear. It didn't matter if my thoughts were, oh, let's say 75 percent crazy. How could I ever tell someone about my fears unless I knew them really, really well? And how could I ever get to know someone really well if there was going to be such weird things to encounter along the way?

For the next few years, I could sometimes charm women and get them to go on dates with me. But I could never be completely honest about who I was or how I was feeling, moment-to-moment, which made it hard to feel close and progress within a relationship.

The scene with Mindy at homecoming became the template for many other encounters, many other times when I would have to interrupt everything with a girl to run as far away as I could to find some bathroom where she wouldn't hear me!

So, in terms of girls: 11th grade – nothing.

12th grade – almost nothing. I had a girlfriend for a very short time. I was crazy about her. We got kind of close. Then she dumped me.

Freshmen year of college, I had a fling with someone – let's call her Ariel – but it never really took off.

This relationship was interesting because it resulted in me getting busted for abusing my Tourette's in a way that was pretty cheesy. I had been experimenting with fake-ticcing words like "kiss-kiss-you" when I liked a girl. When she heard me, I'd pretend to be all embarrassed and say, "Oh! Oh, sorry." If she didn't tell me off, then bingo, I'd have broken the barrier between us. I admit it was horrible and immature to abuse the fact that I had Tourette's, but I only did this a few times, and it was only with women I would be afraid to talk to otherwise.

I had gotten together with Ariel this way. When she later realized I'd been faking it, she got pretty mad at me. She said, "You are so sleazy, by the way. I can't believe you used that one on me. Come on! Give me a break."

Not my finest hour.

Moving on: sophomore year – nothing.

Finally, junior year, I met Elsa. She was definitely the first woman I ever loved. Over the course of our relationship, piece by piece, bit by bit, I had told her about my childhood health issues. She had seen my scars. I was very open about that. But I hadn't pooped around her, and I was still scared to relax and be myself. No way.

One night we were in her bed, and I decided it was time. I was at her dorm, and it was the night before Thanksgiving break. She was going home for break, so we weren't going to be seeing each other for a while. We wanted to spend time together so I didn't want to leave her to run back to my place and then come back. So I mustered up my courage and said, "Look, I need to tell you something." My level of seriousness was so high, it was almost as if I were about to tell her I was pregnant. "I have to go to the bathroom. And brace yourself. Because it's going to be very, very loud."

And then I did it. After I had finished, I walked back into the room with so much fear. I was convinced it was over. I was positive she would never want to touch me again. Instead, she embraced me and gave me a huge kiss. It was amazing. We talked about it later, and it simply ended up not being a big deal. Eventually, we would sleep at each other's places, and she would hear the horror that is me, going to the bathroom. It was never totally comfortable, but it was better than lying and hiding. It was a truly, truly great change in my life. At that point I began to gain the first real insight that my fears were in my own head. My poops didn't change, but my attitude did.

It was still tough trying to have a normal relationship. When Elsa and I were together, I would tic other girls' names constantly. I'd tic words like "ugly!" I'd tic "you're fat" even though I was totally crazy about my girlfriend. She wasn't fat and she was gorgeous – I was totally attracted to her. She knew about Tourette's, but that didn't mean it didn't bother her. There were other issues, too, the kind of issues that any two normal people have, but my Tourette's didn't help. Eventually we broke up.

I was devastated. The breakup coincided with my MCAT struggles. It seemed obvious that I would never get into med school and equally obvious that I would never find anyone else who would accept me. I sucked. At least, that's what I felt at the time. It was a tough stretch for me.

I kept taking practice MCAT tests, trying to work within the standard amount of time. No matter how much I worked at it, I couldn't raise my score. It became clear that taking the test again wasn't going to help anything. Most of my friends were already applying to med schools so that in the fall, a year later, they could enter school. I applied too, but I knew that I wasn't going to be able to get into a very good school. To make matters worse, my year off had already started but my speaking career hadn't.

I decided that getting a degree from a mediocre med school would be better than getting no degree at all. I could always transfer to a better school or prove myself after I became a doctor. I could still become the best doctor ever. Who cared about the stupid degree? I applied to a school in Mexico, another in Tel Aviv and a third one on the Caribbean island of Grenada, called St. George. I even applied to a few D.O. (Doctor of Osteopathy) schools, which are easier to get into but not quite as reputable as regular med schools. I just wanted to make sure I got in somewhere.

As summer ended, I hadn't heard back from any of the schools I'd applied to. My friends were all getting letters inviting them to come interview, which was the second step of the admissions process. I hadn't gotten a single one. I had aimed at the lowest-level schools in the universe, but I guess I hadn't aimed low enough.

So let me set the stage here: I had poured the last four years of my life into getting accepted into medical school and that goal seemed to be more and more out of reach. I was four months into my year off, and I had only gotten hired for two speaking jobs. Neither had come from my marketing packet. I had only gotten them because I was good friends with the people who hired me. My travel for these gigs was paid for, but there was no actual pay for the job. Time was running out for so-called speaking tour, which wasn't very encouraging because I was relying on my successes as a speaker to get into medical school. Things weren't looking great. I found out later that my mom kept calling my brother Brian and asking him if he could intervene. My whole family was beginning to wonder if I had a plan – any plan.

Luckily, my friend Ali who was attending Tufts University had proposed making a documentary film about me, my disorder and my "speaking tour." I said sure, except for the fact that I hadn't gotten any gigs yet and was basically sitting around in my underwear all day, watching a lot of MSNBC. That was my speaking tour that I had pinned so many hopes upon. It was the middle of September. I had nothing else going on. I had taken time off with the goal of doing things, and I wasn't really doing anything. The friend flew me to Boston so she and her classmates could shoot me there.

One day we went to a library and other public places for her to record people's reactions to me and my tics. We went into a McDonald's for lunch. As we ate, I was ticcing, as usual, and two tables away, a group of kids began to stare and laugh at me. It went on and on, this uncontrollable laughing. She got out her camera and started to film the kids. They couldn't stop themselves.

It was painful, obviously, but in the end, it turned out to be great for me. I was able to include the video in my marketing package. It added the perfect touch.

After sitting around my parents' house for a few months, being lazy and depressed, I asked my friend Andreas to help me. He was also applying to medical schools and had done well on his MCAT, but, like my other friends, Andreas was taking a year off from the school grind. Together, we made a list of 150 private schools around the country. Andreas, or Dreas, as I called him, was going to work like an agent for me and take a commission on any gigs he landed.

Now, there were several problems with this plan. Dreas had never worked as an agent before. He'd never worked in sales either, for that matter. He'd worked on a political campaign and proven that he wasn't too bad on the phone. But he knew almost nothing about what he was doing, and I knew even less. Between us, we were clueless. So, with zero skills, we created a website and began to cold-call schools and send off the marketing package across the country.

I vividly remember sitting in my family room at the computer desk with Dreas, dressed in my professional attire of that time: no shirt and my boxers. When Dreas picked up the phone to make the very first call, I was electrified. I felt like we were impostors, or con men, breaking the law by presenting ourselves as mature, grown people offering something real: me! What happened when people found out that we were completely full of it?

After a couple of calls, Dreas began to get the hang of it. What he was saying about me and my presentation suddenly began to seem reasonable. People stayed on the line with him. Within maybe half a dozen calls, people were asking about prices, dates and transportation details.

On the second day, Dreas called a school in upstate Wisconsin. It was a 15-minute phone call. By the time he hung up, he had sealed a deal. We were ecstatic! This was the first positive thing to happen in my life for many, many months.

Eventually, between the efforts of Dreas, me, and another friend, Tara, who was helping us, I had gigs confirmed in Milwaukee, Connecticut, Massachusetts, New York, Illinois, and Washington, D.C. A few more came along in California. Soon there were 20 speaking jobs lined up before the end of the school year.

I felt like I was in a dream. A year earlier, I had this idea, a faint thought in my head about traveling around the country to speak. Now, I had 20 engagements set up in which complete strangers around the country were not only allowing me to speak, but were paying me to come speak to their school. As exhilarating as it was, I was also incredibly scared because it meant I would be held accountable. No one had ever paid me before so if I was horrible, who cared? If I was nervous and sweat through my shirt, I could walk away with no shame because I wasn't a professional "speaker." But, all of a sudden, everything changed.

I would really have to hone my speech. I couldn't just wing it. Now I had to put my feet to the fire and create a meaningful presentation. It's one thing to sell a speech on tolerance but another thing entirely to create a speech with impact.

Suddenly, I was a guy on the move. Over an eight-week period, from February 17 to the end of April, I was rushing from one airport to another. I had flown a lot before in my life because, as an airline employee, my mom had always been able to get us free or cheap tickets. But where previously I had been this annoying guy with Tourette's, suddenly my Tourette's was the reason I was on the plane. I was a guy with a purpose.

I still did what I had always done, which was to announce to the people on the plane that I had Tourette's and tell them not to worry about my tics. But it felt different now. If someone inquired or made small talk after my announcement, I suddenly had the right to say, "Ahem. I'm a speaker on Tourette's."

The speeches were paying maybe $500 each, after expenses like plane fare, food, taxis and the commission I was paying to my "agent." To say the whole thing was low-budget would be an overstatement. Usually, I knew someone in a city near wherever I was speaking, so that's where I'd stay – on the couch. I lived like a vagabond, jumping from a car to a train to a plane to a taxi to another plane, finding one person's house, losing my way every other gig, desperate to find the school where I was supposed to speak, meeting one stranger after another and forgetting many of their names. I had no routine. I was constantly on the move. I was on a bed in Manhattan, in the Bronx, in Stamford, Connecticut, or in San Francisco. It was hectic.

Each time I spoke, I'd sweat through my shirt. I was doing my laundry anywhere I could – at my friends' houses, at Laundromats. One time the airline lost my suitcase and I didn't have anything appropriate to wear. It was a mess.

None of this mattered. I was ecstatic. I had been hoping for so long to do this, and finally it was happening. I was getting paid to travel and meet people! I was getting paid and getting recognition for talking about my challenges. It was the biggest thrill of my life.

The night before the first official gig of my tour was the most nerve-wracking night of my life. For the past year and a half, I had been pretending like I had my act together and like public speaking was going to get me into medical school. This was the key to the life I wanted so badly. But there was one problem: I'd never really put an official speech together.

It's embarrassing to admit, but I'd improvised every speech I'd given up until this point. I was such a perfectionist, and I had such high expectations of myself, that even if it makes no sense, I could never just sit down and work out my speech. If this sounds immature, it's because it was. And now I was furious with myself for such immaturity.

I had my story. And I had plenty of ideas. But having a lot of ideas isn't nearly the same as having one usable idea or having a plan. I had no plan. I hadn't practiced. I hadn't rehearsed. I had no idea how to time my speech. I had no control over whether my speech would be too short or way too long.

I improvised. I did OK. I didn't suck. I let this go on for my first five speeches. It was nerve-wracking. Over the years, I'd talked about different things. I'd talked about my challenges. Thanks to my brother, I'd incorporated a lot of ideas about advocacy in my talk. I'd talked about accepting oneself. I'd focused my speech to be about tolerance. But it was still too broad of an idea. Or at least, my approach to it was still too complicated.

Around this time, I stumbled across a book called "Made to Stick." One of the main points it stressed is simplicity. It repeated itself dozens of times: If you want to communicate to people, make it simple! If you're doing public speaking, make it simple! I realized that I needed to wrap my entire speech around a single, simple idea. I could tell stories of how people had been intolerant, like during the Greyhound incident. Or how they had been understanding, like the black cop during the Greyhound incident. I could explain things I'd learned about myself. I could tell stories I was beginning to hear from people I would meet at speeches. But all of it had to somehow be focused around one basic idea: How can we learn to be more tolerant?

At some point during all of this, I remembered something my dad had mentioned years before, which was the phrase "live and let live." It really struck a chord with me. It was just a simple phrase, but I loved it because it referred to an action, not this vague, abstract idea of "tolerance."

I decided to focus everything in my speech entirely on this one idea. The idea hit me the night before a really big speech I was supposed to deliver in Chicago. It was my 10th speech out of the 20 I had lined up, and it was going to be the biggest audience so far – 1,500 people.

That night, I stayed up late rewriting my speech. I looked backed at all the complicated, painful things I had experienced, and I asked myself, "What is it about this whole experience that might really resonate with other people and express the best of what I've learned?" It was kind of a catalogue of awkward situations. I had to really challenge myself: Why would anyone want to hear about my challenges and the way I conducted myself through them? What was fundamental about my unique experiences that could connect with anyone?

Here I was, this in many ways normal guy who went to public high school, played sports, participated in school theater and student government, and had plenty of friends and a few girlfriends. In many ways, I had had a "successful" childhood. Yet for 20 years of my life, I displayed ridiculous behaviors. Between ticcing some 21 million times and having thousands of super loud, explosive bowel movements, I conveyed an outward appearance that set me apart from almost everyone.

The difference between my problems and other people's problems was simply that mine were so noticeable. Every time people noticed them, which was often, they made assumptions about who I was that had nothing to do with who I was on the inside. Every time I had a hassle because of my disorders; every time I was hurt, upset or annoyed; every time I wasn't tolerated (like the time I got kicked off the Greyhound bus, the time the tennis player's father gave me a hard time, the time the guy almost beat me up at the Japanese restaurant or the time the woman at Wendy's called me retarded), what became clear in each episode was that people were making assumptions about who I was based on a few outward characteristics.

In a matter of seconds, they had ignored who I was on the inside, judged me on some superficial information and made a decision about me: I was a bad guy. Or I was this, or I was that.

But, although the reasons for my experience were different from most people's, my experience of pain and shame wasn't unique. *Because almost everyone has their own "tics" that other people misinterpret and act upon.* And acting upon those misinterpretations, to my mind, is intolerance.

What I would have wanted in those situations – and I imagine this is what anyone with a "tic" or problem wants from the world – is for other people simply to let us be. If people wanted to think I was crazy, taking drugs or possessed by the devil, it would have been totally fine. Anyone can make any assumptions about me or anyone else. Just don't make those assumptions – which are so often harmful, negative and just plain wrong – be the basis for actions that might harm me or have a negative impact on me. So that's what I decided to capture with the phrase "Live and Let Live."

I rewrote my entire speech around this one single idea. If it didn't have anything to do with "Live and Let Live," it was out. I kept making changes to the speech, even in the car ride to the school, right up until the last minute.

It worked.

When I finished sharing my "Live and Let Live" approach, I got a standing ovation.

I had never seen or felt anything like it. My speeches before hadn't been horrible. But they had never been great. This was different. Fifteen hundred people were standing up and clapping about whatever had just come out of my mouth. I'd be lying if I said I didn't totally bask in the glory. I have never felt so humbled before.

Not only did people enjoy the speech, they accepted me and my struggle. I'd found a way to use my Tourette's and Hirschsprung's as tools to reach out to people and talk about something much more universal than just me. All of the embarrassment I had ever felt had proven useful as a tool to help reach out to other people and help them feel better about their own problems. I felt completely awed and proud.

For the rest of my 20 speeches, I framed my presentation in terms of "Live and Let Live." I got several more standing ovations.

After a little more than 60 days of travel, 17 different cities and 16 couches and beds, I was finally back in the comfort of my own bed. Over the course of two months, I had spoken to approximately 5,000 individuals

But I hadn't gotten a single interview with even one med school.

Somewhere, around March of that year, I'd decided to take another year off before med school. In retrospect, this was beyond a cry for help and plainly ridiculous. I had no more speaking gigs lined up. I had no interviews arranged with any med school in the universe. What was I taking a year off from, exactly? From nothing.

Back in Clayton, I started working as a substitute teacher. I needed money. I was living at home with my mom. Things were not auspicious.

Finally, one day I got an email, and there it was: an invitation for a med school interview in New York. I won't mention the name. But it was one of the less-ambitious choices of all the schools I had applied to. It was a D.O. school, which, like I said, qualifies as a medical school but is easier to get into. And it was my only chance.

I had a speaking job lined up at a high school in New Jersey. I planned to use this gig to pay for my travel from St Louis to meet with the school officials in New York. But I planned everything wrong: My speech went so late that I crashed at a friend's house near the school where I was interviewing. Unfortunately, my suit was at another friend's apartment, 100 blocks south. At night, I gave a wonderful, uplifting speech. But the next day, I didn't have time to get my suit. I had had such a positive experience speaking to the audience of about 350 people. Surely this was more important than whether I had a suit, right?

I walked through the doors of the school. In the waiting room, there were a dozen or so applicants, all looking very serious, wearing suits and ties. And there I was in jeans and a sweater.

It was a horrible interview. It was like tooth extraction. Finally, the interviewer let me have it. He said to me, "You've been hoping to be a doctor your whole life. You say that you're serious. Everything you've done your whole life has been to prepare for this moment. Why the hell are you here, wearing jeans?"

I tried to explain to him about my speaking engagement and my impossible schedule.... And then it hit me ...

"I don't want to be a doctor anymore."

I swear to God, until that moment, my conscious dream was to go to med school.

By the time I walked out, I knew the truth: I hadn't wanted to be a doctor for quite a while. I had totally replaced that dream with a much better one. I already had a way to have a positive impact in the world. "Duh!" The speeches! Tolerance! I already had my life's work cut out for me.

I left the school and took the subway down to Times Square, made my way to the airport and flew back to St. Louis.

My whole future had rewritten itself in front of me like a pop-up book: I was going to move to New York. I was going to become a professional speaker. Oh yes, and finally, in September 2009, after I'd moved to New York to do just that, not only did I get an interview, I got accepted to a med school in the Caribbean called St. George's. Too late. I had already set out to become America's most offensive proponent of tolerance!

I've been traveling the country speaking about tolerance for about three years. I have to pinch myself a few times a week to make sure I'm not dreaming because sometimes it seems so unreal. I have booked more than 200 engagements in 37 states, Canada and Central America. I've spoken to approximately 100,000 people. My website links to the 10-minute documentary my friends from Tufts made. It's been viewed on YouTube by more than 250,000 people around the world. And in February 2011, I was voted College Speaker of the Year and Diversity Speaker of the Year by *Campus Activities Magazine.*

I've received emails from all over the world, from Greece to Argentina, Hungary to China, from people who found my message helpful, even inspirational. A woman in Finland mailed me a video of herself doing an interpretative dance about Tourette's! (People say thank you in all sorts of ways.)

I think that the reason people respond to me is not because of my life or my problems. Certainly, most of them don't have Tourette's or Hirschsprung's disease. They're responding to my idea of "Live and Let Live."

My speech has gone through many changes since that night in Chicago. But as I get a better understanding of myself through all of the people I meet on the road, I'm realizing that the core of my thinking remains the same: We know so little about other people. We really don't have any idea what makes them tic.

I don't want to make the assumption that anyone reading this book has seen me speak or seen my video so, at the risk of repeating something you already have heard, let me explain a bit more about what I mean.

When I say "Live and Let Live,"' what I mean is tolerance. Not "acceptance," just tolerance. There's a difference between the two, and tolerance, to me, is the easier, more attainable goal to aim for, the simplest, beginner's-level method of getting along. It doesn't mean we love everyone and force ourselves to smile at everyone and think everyone is great. It just refers to the bare minimum of how we should treat people. And by that I mean raising our awareness and being honest about how little we know about others. Let me give some examples.

Last spring, I was in California speaking at an incredibly exclusive private school. It had an extremely beautiful outdoor amphitheater overlooking some foothills. You couldn't have picked a place with more successful, beautifully dressed, healthy-looking people with all the advantages of our society.

After I finished speaking, people came up to the stage to say hi or say thanks or tell stories. Four kids were kind of hanging back from the rest. I'd seen this before. They had something they wanted to say, and they were waiting until the others left so they could feel comfortable telling me what was on their mind. As soon as the others left, they told me their stories. The first, a girl, was dealing with anorexia; the second, a guy, had Crohn's disease, a serious, life-impairing bowel disorder; the third kid had an ileostomy (a bag outside her stomach that collected her poop, like I had when I was a baby). And the fourth had been mentally and physically abused by her mother for years. This girl had taken her mother to court and petitioned to be emancipated. During the prolonged court process, she missed an incredible amount of school, and when she was able to make it to school, she was usually in a horrible mood. She told me how students thought she was the "crazy" girl, how her other family members barely understood her situation and how they couldn't believe she would take her mother to court. This was just one school out of the many, many schools I now visit routinely.

I met a couple from Bolivia a few months ago. They told me they'd been having the hardest time here in the United States. No one can understand them. I'll be honest: It was hard for me to understand them, too! English is not their first language, and they're just learning how to speak it. And what happens to them all the time is that people misunderstand them and often think they're completely incompetent, despite the fact that both of them are enrolled in higher learning institutions earning degrees.

Last spring, while speaking at college in the mid-Atlantic, a girl waited to talk to me. I'll say it as plainly as I can: She was incredibly fat. Huge. After everyone had scattered, she gave me an enormous smile and asked, "Marc, take a guess what my problem is?" I chuckled because it was obviously a test. I had no idea for sure what her "problem" might be, but I assumed it must have something to do with her weight. Her answer blew me away: "I'm bulimic." For something like 10 years, this incredibly fat girl had been throwing up her food. But people continually gave her a hard time about her weight.

What is common among all these stories is that all of these people had some challenge or quirk in their life and displayed certain characteristics – a tic, let's call it (erratic behavior at school, poor communication schools, obesity and so on). The people around them had made assumptions about who they were as people, without really knowing the true story.

Now, I need to emphasize an important aspect of "Live and Let Live." Making assumptions and judgments about other people is totally OK. It's natural. We need to make decisions about people and situations on a gut level in order to survive. And we do it all the time. In fact, if I were to judge people for doing it, I would, in fact, be hypocritically judging other people for being judgmental. So really, there's no criticism on my part about the fact that we all do this. But my big concern is and always has been how we proceed *after* making a judgment or an assumption.

What marks a behavior as intolerant, and therefore, destructive, is when people turn assumptions or judgmental thoughts into action. When people assume they understand my "tics" or other people's "tics," and then act – by kicking me off a bus, by calling me retarded, by laughing at me. That's where they crossed the line from judgment to intolerance.

Obviously, there are times in life when a person has to act on their negative assumptions. Should you ignore it if you're on a plane and the person next to you starts to light something that looks like a bomb? How about if you're black and you're walking around in a very white area known for heavy Ku Klux Klan membership and someone starts calling you the n-word? In these situations, where one fears one's own safety, there is clearly a line of judgment that needs to be acknowledged where tolerance is not the answer so much as self-protection. I'm not going to define where that line is, but I'll trust for now that it's a fairly clear one.

At its most fundamental level, "Live and Let Live" means knowing when and how to recognize that most of what we think about others is just an assumption. "Live and Let Live" is easy to say but incredibly hard to do, especially because many of us have never tried it and don't have much practice with it. We've never really even thought about it. But imagine the following examples:

You see a girl on the street who's fat. You think: "Why doesn't she have more self-control?"

What about the kid who raises his hand too often in class? "Geek. Doesn't he ever get tired of showing off?"

Let's say there's some girl you used to be kind of friendly with. And now she never talks to you. What do you think about her? She's rude! She's snotty, right?

We dismiss these people with one or two words or thoughts. "They suck." "They're rude." "What a loser." Of course, most of us, most of the time, don't say these thoughts out loud. But we sure spend plenty of time thinking them.

We walk down the hallway at school and we pass by the jock, the prude, the nerd, the loser, the druggy, the fox. We made up our minds a long time ago about them – all of them.

The jock is happy and maybe kind of simple. The prude is stuck-up or prissy for no good reason. The nerd doesn't have emotions. The loser is disgusting and has nothing to offer. The druggy is, well, druggy. The fox doesn't have any problems at all.

But if we slow down to think about each of these people, one at a time, we have to ask ourselves: "What do I actually *know* about this person?"

Take the example of the fat girl. Do you know whether she's working three part-time jobs and simply doesn't have time to make it to the gym? Or, as I learned in real life, what if she's actually bulimic and has a metabolism disorder?

How about the hand-raiser? Do you know what's going on in that kid's house? Does his father beat him? Oh, you don't know that, either!

How about the jock? Is he an incest victim? Oh, you never actually talked to him before. Interesting!

And what about the girl who used to be friendly with you but who now seems aloof and doesn't talk much? Is it possible her parents are getting a divorce? What if one of her parents is really, really sick, and she's depressed? Are you still so mad at her for not talking to anyone?

I've met all of these people. They're real. And chances are excellent that you've met them, too. They're all around you. Every day. My job simply gives me the benefit of being able to meet them and talk with them. I'm just in a position where they come up to me and tell me about themselves and how they suffer from intolerance.

Again and again, what I see is how little we know about the people we judge. We see a few details, we decide that we know what their situation is, and then, instead of having compassion and recognizing that every person has their own story – their own tics – we react.

After my speeches, people often say to me, "Marc, I will never judge someone again." This statement is hilarious to me for many reasons, but most notably because we're only human; no speech by me or anyone else is going to stop people from making snap judgments about other people. But what has been gratifying to me is to sense that, when I bring my message to people, an incredible shift occurs. As people begin seeing their assumptions as just assumptions, they naturally get a deeper understanding of why it's so important to "Live and Let Live." And they realize, "This isn't about being a good person or a bad person. It's about being a calmer person. A happier person." If nothing else, it's about saving our brainpower for more useful activities.

I spoke at Bowdoin College once, and this kid came up to me. He seemed like a normal, cool college kid. He confessed to me: "There's this kid who sits by me in science class. He has this weird way of breathing. He's really awkward and noisy. And I've been laughing at him non-stop for months."

This kid from Bowdoin shook his head and asked, "Why am I laughing at this kid? I don't even know what's going on with him. I realized after hearing you speak: why am I so consumed with someone else's life? If I Live and Let Live, I can just relax and worry, or God forbid, enjoy my own life and focus on what's in front of me!"

He said it better than I could. "Instead of wasting all this energy judging other people for their weaknesses or their habits that seem strange to me, what if I just, you know, smell the roses or enjoy the weather, or whatever? Life's too short for me to waste my time, filling my head with all this negative crap about everyone else's life! Why should I waste my time sneering at some kid for the way he breathes? I'm not hurting him. I'm hurting me."

When we get wrapped up in making judgments, and making decisions about who people are, and deciding what's wrong with them, or that they suck, or that they're losers, we fill our minds with garbage. In the end, who does it hurt? Well, many times, we hurt the people around us by making wrong assumptions about them. But we also hurt ourselves. Because we're the ones walking around with the negative energy, the negative thoughts.

One payoff you get when you really learn to Live and Let Live is that you get more power. You stop living in a fantasy world where you think you know things that you don't. Instead of spending all your energy festering on other people's weaknesses, you have more energy to look at yourself or look at life. It's much less stressful. You have much more freedom and energy to enjoy the scenery.

So the next time you feel that judgmental voice saying, "Ugh! Douchebag!" or "What a loser!," I want you to slow down and stop.

Right there.

We like to protect ourselves by "knowing" things. I put "know" in quotes. The truth is, so many of the things we think we know turn out to be false. Or, at least, more complicated than we thought they were.

There's a quote I read once that says: "The more I learn, the more I realize I don't know." It's true. Wisdom consists more often than not of understanding how little we know. It consists of being comfortable admitting that fact and taking the time to learn things before we make judgments.

We're so used to filling in the blanks, filling in the story about everyone we know – and even people we don't know so well. "Oh my God, I know him. I know her. She's a bitch. He sucks. He's Spanish. Spanish people are this. Jews are that. Rich people are this. Democrats are this. I know what's going on in their life."

The moment we learn how to recognize this judgment and say, "Oh, wait. I don't know," and take a deep breath or two and wait it out, that's what we call a teachable moment. That's the moment when we take about 10 steps forward in learning how to Live and Let Live.

You might need to circle back to the same lesson again and again. But you can never go wrong by hitting the mental "pause button" whenever you think you know what makes people tic.

One of my favorite quotes – often attributed to Plato – ties up this idea beautifully: "Be kinder than necessary, for everyone you meet is fighting some kind of battle."

At the end of July 2009, I left St. Louis and my parents and brought three duffel bags to New York. I moved in with my brother Brian. It was a pretty spontaneous decision. I just wanted to see what it would be like to live in the most intense city in the United States, and what could be safer than living with a family member to help show me the ropes?

He told me later that he worried I might be a little too "frat-tastic" for him. By this he meant that I might be too immature or act like a party boy.

Brian had just gotten out of Harvard Business School, and he had this amazing job working for an international non-profit. Here I was with a couple thousand dollars and only a very few speaking gigs lined up. I had borrowed some money to finance this new dream, but I only had enough to last until December. So, on top of everything else, Brian worried I wouldn't even be able to pay my rent.

It was exciting to arrive in New York City, and even more so to live with my brother. I had been living at my mother's house, back in Clayton, in suburban St. Louis, which is a fairly slow-paced lifestyle. But suddenly, I was living in the busiest city in the country, with one of the most ambitious, motivated people I've ever known.

It was a steep learning curve for me. Brian helped me learn how to think and work like an adult, like a professional. I had come to New York to become a professional speaker. But he would catch me on Craigslist, looking for part-time jobs as a babysitter or a substitute teacher. I was fixated on getting some short-term cash because I was worried about running out of money.

Brian got me to focus and have confidence in my goal. He made me realize that if I spent 10 hours a week as a bartender or something unrelated to my dream – instead of 10 hours a week trying to book speaking gigs – I was taking myself out of the game, sabotaging myself. I needed to maintain my main thrust in life. I needed to take a chance and give it some time to pay off. He pushed me to hire someone to make sales calls for me because that wasn't my strong point. I did, and she turned out to be awesome.

Before long, however, Brian started working on a big idea of his own for a non-profit. Soon, in addition to the full-time job he already had, he was coming home and working another 40 to 50 hours researching and fund-raising. He was quite literally working a hundred hours a week. This went on for months. So there we were, two brothers, both starting their own business. And it was great – except I never got to see my brother anymore!! I missed him. We had very little social life.

I had even less of a romantic life. Of course, this had long been a problematic area for me. A few years ago, during a college speech, the subject of romance came up, and someone asked me, "Marc, can you have sex like everyone else?" And I answered, "It's not like my penis has Tourette syndrome!"

That got a big laugh.

But the truth is that my relationship problems had persisted for so long that I began to wonder if maybe I was gay.

My insecurity, self-doubt, lack of experience and, probably more than anything, my OCD, made me very nervous about this subject. I would ask myself over and over again, "Are you sure you aren't gay? Maybe you're just gay!" And I'd answer myself, "Umm, I don't think so. I'm not attracted to guys. I love girls!" And that same voice would say, "Oh, nice. You're defensive. Why are you so defensive if you're not gay?"

The summer before my junior year of college, I had grown desperate about being a virgin. Every one of my friends had had sex but me. I felt like something must be – or at least, might be – wrong with me.

There was a girl with whom I used to have a "friends with benefits" arrangement in high school, and she happened to be coming back to St. Louis for summer vacation. I called her up one day and asked her very directly and honestly: Would she help me out with my situation? I needed to get it over with. It was time. She was very sweet. She answered right away, "Yeah! Totally!" So, the day before my 21st birthday, I ended up losing my virginity. It was awesome.

And even though everything had felt very natural with her, I still underwent this endless self-doubt, this endless internal reasoning and debating, as if I had to prove to myself as well as the world that I wasn't gay. Why would any sane person have to prove anything to anybody? I don't know now. But at the time, the same thoughts kept looping around my head, around and around. "Wait a minute, Marc, you're not gay. You know you're not gay! Oh yeah? How do you know? Obviously, you wouldn't be so worried if there wasn't anything to worry about!" In the same way that I used to fixate on sticking my hand down the garbage disposal, it wasn't something you can explain. It was intense, as if I was trying to hurt myself and push this thought harder and harder until it became destructive. This is the magic of OCD.

I made an assumption that, when I went to go live with my brother, I was going to get a closer look at what gay life was like and probably get a chance to learn about myself. It turned out that this was one time my assumption was right!

When Brian did have friends over, they were mostly gay guys. After watching them hanging out, one thing became perfectly clear to me: I was not like them. I wasn't gay. My OCD mind had been telling me to worry – and worry and worry – about being gay, but when I saw gay men talking about other men sexually, it was very simple: I knew that I didn't identify with that. They talked about other guys the same way my straight guy friends and I would talk about girls. Their conversations didn't quite make sense to me – because I wasn't gay! I'm sure if I were gay, it would have made perfect sense. In the end, it was as silly as if my OCD had been telling me I was a rhinoceros. I had been worried about nothing.

By living with Brian, I saw for myself how little I knew about being gay. It was incredibly humbling. It had been 10 years since Brian had come out, and yet I really knew very little about gay people. It was like learning about another culture; in fact, it *was* another culture. It was yet another reminder of how little I know about other people's lives – including someone as close to me as my brother.

This kind of humbling awareness happened more and more as I traveled throughout the school year. I met so many new people with endlessly illuminating stories. These people had problems, large and small, that played out in all kinds of ways that I never could have imagined.

I was speaking at a community college in Atlanta when I met this really sweet girl. She looked so innocent, perky and healthy it was scary. It turned out that, by the time she was 18 years old, she had already gone a few rounds with serious drugs, such as heroin and coke. She had been through drug rehab. When I met her, she was on this awareness committee to help other people cope with addiction. She was an amazing reminder, yet again, that you simply never know what someone's been through.

Another girl I met recently revealed to me in private that she's a cutter. How would I have known if she didn't tell me directly?

I remember back when I was at Washington University, and many of the lawn care guys were Hispanic. There was a guy I passed by a lot, and we got into the habit of saying hello. One day he asked me to tutor him in English.

Before I'd actually known him, I had made a whole set of assumptions. I thought he was probably a peasant farmer from somewhere in the country, a *campesino*. Weren't most Mexican illegal immigrants impoverished farmers who couldn't earn a decent living in the countryside, no matter how hard they worked? It turned out I was completely wrong. The guy was a doctor in his home country and was trying to work his way back up the ladder in the United States. He had a better education than I had. (Later I even wondered what *he* would have gotten on his MCAT? Maybe a higher score than I had!)

I *still* find myself making assumptions about people. I recently met a beautiful girl at a community college in Ohio. Her name was Tani. I assumed she was Indian, but I wasn't sure. She had beautiful skin. We ended up on a sort of accidental date. (OK, I thought she was pretty, so it wasn't that accidental.) We were talking, and I realized, "Hmm. Her way of talking doesn't seem very educated. She's studying at a pretty humdrum, unglamorous school. She can't be that smart."

I was wrong – on so many counts. She was from Bangladesh, her dad was an engineer, her mom was something else fairly fancy and high-functioning back in Bangladesh, and her family moved to the States with nothing. Her dad worked as a custodian to provide for her. She was paying for everything – tuition, room and board – on her own, and she had this incredible grasp on life. In her spare time, she was a mentor for a girl who had Down syndrome!

I write this not to suggest that I'm a horrible person for making these assumptions but to emphasize again how far our assumptions can be from the truth.

The best story I ever heard about why we should Live and Let Live was on a subway in New York. It was December 2009, and I was waiting at the subway station on 23rd Street for the A train. I had my headphones on, and I was swaying to the music a bit, kind of dancing. It goes without saying that I was also sniffing, chomping my teeth and barking a little. Not as bad as sometimes but enough perhaps to scare someone.

There was a guy a few feet away from me. Even though I don't always do this, I thought, "Well, I'm in the subway. I better err on the side of caution." So I said, "Sir, I have Tourette syndrome. I just wanted to give you a heads-up."

He gave me a look and a hand signal, like, "Dude, no worries. I'm cool." I guess it was the way he gave me the hand signal – he was clearly so much more relaxed than most people. It was striking. I decided I wanted to find out why he was so cool and relaxed. So I approached him and asked, "Sir, I know this is really bizarre, but what were you thinking about me before I told you that I had Tourette's?"

He was a skinny, Hispanic-looking guy – bald, maybe 28 or 30. He said, "Honestly? I just thought you were having a really good time."

So I kind of laughed and asked him, "Um, OK, but what about when I started to chomp my teeth?"

He smiled and said, "Well, yes, that was weird."

He introduced himself, and I learned that his name was Jay. The conversation between Jay and me continued all the way to 160th Street, about 25 minutes. I got the chance to press him a little further: "You saw me there, chomping and sniffing. I could tell you were mellower about it than most people. What is it that makes you one of the mellow people? Why didn't you get rattled by it? Why did you seem so calm about my weird behavior?"

He said: "Well, Marc, it's funny you ask that. When I was 16 years old, I was on the back of a bus in New York City, and up in front, there was this screaming, annoying kid sitting next to his dad. Everyone on the bus started getting annoyed. The kid was really going nuts, just whining and whining, acting like a little monster – way beyond normal. And the dad wasn't doing anything. He was just letting the kid get away with it. Everyone on the bus was really surprised because it was just offensive. This woman sitting next to me started to get really pissed, and she was just fuming. 'If that was my kid, I'd shut him up good!'

"Another person started complaining, and finally, some guy got up from his seat and walked up to the dad. Speaking for everyone on the bus, he said, 'Will you *please* control your kid?'

"And the dad turned to the stranger and said, 'I'm sorry. His mother just died. We're coming from the funeral.'

"At that moment, I realized: I don't know anything about anybody. I don't know what people are thinking. I don't know what people are doing. I decided I just need to let people be."

I've never heard a better example of why we should all Live and Let Live, and I immediately started using Jay's story in my speeches. Pretend you're in this situation. You're in public somewhere and you hear a kid crying. It's perfectly fine to approach and see if everything's OK. The point is to do so with an open mind, rather than assuming something that might be false and causing additional, unintended pain. There's nothing wrong with simply asking, "Hey is your kid OK?" Just don't assume you know anything about the situation before you ask. Because you probably don't.

I often ask students in the audience to think of a challenge they have that is weighing on them. I tell them to look around, first at a stranger and then at someone close to them. Then I ask them: "Have you ever thought for a moment that the person you really knew or maybe that total stranger at school woke up with the exact same challenge as you did this morning?"

Just like that little boy on the bus, how much do we really know about each other's lives and what we go through on a day-to-day basis? Do you really know about the person who just cut you off in traffic? Do you really know why someone at work is being rude to you? That kid who wears horrible clothes, the girl who's such a know-it-all, the loser with bad breath – do you have any idea if their father just lost his job? Or if their mom is a drunk? Do you really know what makes them tic?

I was on cloud nine after meeting Jay. I was an inspirational speaker on tolerance and I had just met this incredible guy who had given me the perfect addition to my speech. After I added it, I felt like I had taken my message to a whole new level. People continued to be blown away by the speech – at least when I delivered it well. I couldn't have been happier. Everything was perfect.

A few months later, I met a man named Daniel Packard. Daniel happened to be another speaker on the college circuit. We were introduced at a conference in Portland, Oregon, and quickly became friends. A few months after we met, we ran into each other at the Chattanooga airport. We were walking through the airport together when I realized I needed to fill up my water bottle. I asked Daniel to wait for me. When I returned, I said, "Sorry you had to wait."

And he replied, "Marc, you know what? You are the biggest hypocrite I know."

I was sort of taken aback, but, before I could react, he asked me why I apologized to him.

I replied that I felt bad that he had to wait for me.

Then he asked me: "Why do you think I would care if you took 30 seconds to get some water?"

He wasn't trying to get on my case, but he pointed out that it was kind of unusual how many times I'd said "sorry" during the brief time we'd known each other. I realized he was right. It was a long-standing pattern: I've been saying "I'm sorry" my whole life. If I barely bump into someone, if I forget to hold the door for someone or interrupt a conversation – I apologize.

He asked me, "Would you agree that you're apologizing because you think people are hard on you and you're trying to make sure they won't think negative things about you?"

I gulped and said, yes, that was probably right.

"Marc, do you know why a pathological liar thinks everyone they interact with is lying?"

I shrugged.

"Because they always lie," he continued. "And when they look out into the world through their lens, they think everyone is also lying. Do you see the logic? If you think everyone is being hard on you, what's really happening? Could it just be that you're being hard on yourself instead?"

It hit me like a hundred-pound weight: There I was, going around the country, telling people to Live and Let Live and be tolerant of others, and yet I didn't even tolerate myself.

Up to that moment, I had never looked at my life in that way. As we talked more and more, I began to have a deeper understanding of the suffering I had actually caused myself through my own intolerance. I looked back to my past and got some very painful insights.

I thought of all the times I told everyone I had TS. I would make all my announcements to people, warning everyone in the world that I had Tourette's – at airports, sports games, waiting in line at Starbucks, fast-food joints or on the platform of the subway, to name a few. My friends would say, "Marc, you don't need to tell everyone that you have TS." And I would insist, "No! They do care! People really do care! I have been kicked off a bus! Believe me, they care!" And yes, some people do care. But to think that everyone in the world cares is kind of crazy. I actually never knew what strangers thought of me. I just assumed they were uncomfortable with my noises; I assumed that making an announcement to explain my situation would put them more at ease. But suddenly I began to see the picture more clearly: The person who cared the most, the person who was judging my condition the most, was me!

I had felt that if I could get people to understand me, they would see that beneath all my strange behavior, I was really a normal guy. And then they would accept me. And then I would be happy. At times, I had even told friends, "If everyone in the world knew I had Tourette's, my life would be so much better."

And then I thought about my poops.

Every single time I sat on a toilet in fear of what people in the stall next to me were thinking, I had really thought it was *they* who weren't letting me live my life in peace. Now I see the truth. I thought I was disgusting and weird and assumed that everyone else in the bathroom with me felt the same. My self -judgment prevented me from calmly going to the bathroom in public places, with friends, or around girls.

Of course, the problem with waiting for the world to accept me was that I had basically put my happiness in the hands of other people. It was up to you whether I would be happy. If you didn't accept me, I wasn't going to be happy.

I had spent so much time being so aggressively open about my problems, trying to get the whole world to understand me and my disorders, trying to find happiness through acceptance. But it didn't work. Most people accepted me, some people didn't, but either way, it didn't end up making me happy because, deep down inside, I really didn't tolerate myself.

Thanks to Daniel, I underwent a huge shift in my understanding of tolerance. If we tolerate ourselves, it matters a lot, lot less what other people think of us. Right?

Why would it matter if someone laughed at me or made a crude remark? What if I had just accepted myself and decided not to worry about other people's opinions? Why would I have ever been thinking about the ankles I could see in the bathroom stall next to me or worrying constantly about what my girlfriend thought of me? I would have never needed to get angry or frustrated or mad at someone else. I realized that, not only did I need to let other people live their lives, but I needed to let me live my life. I needed to practice what I preached.

And now, let's bring this discussion back to you. Pick some insecurity that you live with every day. Maybe you think you're too tall, too fat, too skinny, not smart enough or not athletic enough. Imagine for a few seconds that you could be totally OK with that insecurity. Would it matter so much if anyone ever made fun of you? Imagine if you could be OK with yourself and I could be OK with my poops and TS, how much happier would we both be?

It's never easy. I've been thinking about tolerance and what it means and how to apply it to my life for *years,* and it's still not easy. But I keep trying.

I don't know if I'll ever be able to accept myself 100 percent of the way, 100 percent of the time. I don't know if anyone can.

Ever since that discussion with Daniel, step-by-step, I've gotten more comfortable with myself. When I'm dating someone, I'm much more open about things from the very beginning. It's less and less of a big deal. I put much less energy into hiding things. It's still not easy to have a relationship, but it's less because of my health challenges than my work schedule. Maybe I'm a workaholic. Or maybe I'm a workaholic because I feel like, with my disorders, I need to work extra hard. Or maybe I just love my job. I'm not sure.

These days, I fly around all the time. This past spring, I was in 54 cities in 90 days. It makes it tricky to try to have a relationship. For now, I can just say that I'm a work in progress. And it's funny: I can get up on a stage and talk to a thousand people, and I can be so true to who I am. I can exude so much confidence about who I am. I can talk about ticcing and all the embarrassing things I say, and I can talk about pooping liquid poop five to eight times a day.

Yet, it's still sometimes uncomfortable for me around women I'm interested in. I feel like I'm not as casual as many guys my age. Recently I met this gorgeous girl through some friends of mine. She was incredibly smart and fun to be with. At the end of our first date, we ended up back at her house. We were hanging out in the kitchen, talking, and suddenly I started ticcing, "I love you! I love you!" It was an incredibly funny moment. In the past, I probably would have been so embarrassed I would have had to leave. As it was, it launched us into our first kiss. Score one for Tourette's, ladies and gentlemen.

In fall 2010, three of my best friends, Ross, Greg, and Mike suggested that we all live together in Boston. I jumped at the idea. I was traveling so much, I just felt like I wanted to party a bit more when I came home. Or at least have a social life. In New York, my brother was always working. He was doing his thing, and I was doing mine. We barely saw each other. So I moved. Ever since then, I've been flying around the country and coming back to my home in Boston. Every time I come back, I learn something new. And every time I go out on the road, I have something new to share. It's an awesome life.

I was in Wichita, Kansas, at Friends University, doing a presentation. About 90 people were in the audience, and, for some reason, the energy in the room was especially positive. During my speech, someone I couldn't quite see kept coughing really badly. I've given a lot of speeches where people were ticcing. I'm pretty good at not getting distracted. But this time, I couldn't help thinking to myself, "Um, you're distracting people!"

I got through the talk, and afterward a girl came over to say hi. She was very short, maybe about 4 feet, 5 inches. It turned out she has something called Turner syndrome, a chromosomal disorder that causes a growth abnormality.

She had obviously been through a lot and had faced a lot of intolerance and difficulties. But she had this really, really positive attitude. As I listened to her, I finally had to ask, "Where do you derive this sense of joy?"

She said: "Well, I had a very powerful experience last year," and she brought out a picture of her cousin. The cousin had been on a street corner with some friends when someone pushed him into the street. He was hit by a truck and died. Instantly. "You know, I learned that tomorrow is not promised."

I had never heard that phrase before, but it really hit me. She continued, "I want to enjoy my life."

This girl had what I would consider way more health issues than I ever had, and she had chosen to be positive about it. She had clearly made a commitment and a choice to live life as a blessing and not a curse.

As we continued talking, she began to cough. I realized that she had been the one who had been coughing during my presentation. "Sorry about this," she said. "I have really bad asthma as a result of my Turner syndrome."

I almost burst out laughing. Here I was, being Mr. Tolerance speaker, and yet I will always have further to go. I had been slightly frustrated when she kept coughing during my speech. Of course, if I had known her complicated reality, I wouldn't have wasted that energy.

Live and Let Live means I don't need to waste my time judging people and making assumptions about why they do what they do. It also means you can address a situation without demonizing the source of your discomfort. Let's say someone is sitting next to you on a train or a bus or plane, and his earphones are blasting away. Maybe it really *is* rude and distracting, and that is a fact. You're not just being judgmental. It's *loud*. Your initial assumption might be "Oh my God. This person is so annoying. Why doesn't he just shut up? He's so rude!"

Here you have a choice. You can make an assumption that his

intentions are rude and that he doesn't care about you and that he's a selfish, bad person. Or you can realize, "Oh, wait, I don't know anything about this person." Maybe he was fighting in Iraq and suffered hearing damage in a car bomb explosion. Or maybe he has no idea that people around him can hear his music because they're just fuming in resentful silence. Who knows? The point is: You have the right to ask him to turn down the volume. But why bother making assumptions about his intentions? You don't know. But if you simply ask, "Hey, I have very sensitive ears. Would you mind turning your headphone down a bit?" you're going to get a completely different reaction than if you make an assumption that he's a horrible person.

O ver the years, people have come to me with advice about my Tourette's. Lots of advice. I've had people run up to me and tell me that if only I accepted Jesus right then and there, I would get better. I've had people pray for me on an airplane. I've had people tell me about diets and acupuncture. I've had people come up to me at Starbucks and demonstrate yoga positions they insist I should do. I've had people send me videos showing special retainers I could put in my mouth that would supposedly curb my Tourette's.

Some of this advice has been helpful. Some has been outlandish or silly. Over the years, I've also tried various medications, the therapies I describe in this book and even hypnosis. But none of the advice or therapy or medications has worked very well.

Thanks to slowly evolving measures of self-acceptance, I've been able to cope with my Tourette's "itches" in a new way. I still have the same tics and surges I've always had. But I've learned to channel the energy they stir up in a completely new way.

Instead of bouncing off every tic and thinking, "Oh my God! It never stops! I'm going to be suffering from this for ever and ever and ever! When will it ever stop? When will I ever have peace?" I'm able to relax more and be in the moment. More and more often, I'm able to contain each tic and not think of the next and the next. I live in the moment, and sometimes I can even think, "Well, this is just the way it is. This is just the way I am. And I'm fine. My life is fine. If this is part of what it takes to be me, it must be OK."

As a result, my Tourette's has improved. Dramatically. In fact, I've even had weeks in which my Tourette's was virtually gone. Ninety-five percent gone, perhaps. My poops have not become solid – that's never going to happen – but my OCD seems to be lessening where they are concerned, and that is a tremendous relief.

Although my symptoms go up and down, they do seem to be trending toward more manageability. I don't suspect that there is a finish line I will one day cross, where suddenly I will be "normal." In fact, I've realized that if I keep hoping for "someday," then I'm never going to be able to enjoy the present day or the present moment. The idea that there is some perfect moment out there or someday when I won't have problems is an illusion. I'm never going to get there. I can't tell you what a relief it is to me to understand this. It's up to me to enjoy the present moment and let myself Live and Let Live. I have finally gotten to the point where I don't resent the struggle all the time. I accept it. Sometimes, strange as it may seem, I even enjoy it.

I used to think of my life as a marathon. I was running away from my Tourette's, I was running away from my Hirschsprung's. All I could hope for was to get to that fantasy moment where life no longer sucked, where things no longer hurt me, where I no longer felt the pressure of dealing with my disorders, their symptoms, and the reactions they caused.

The main pressure I felt was created by worrying about what other people thought. I almost want to cry when I think of it: It was like being in a house surrounded by rising flood waters. I never lived one moment free from panic because I've always stood out. I've never had the experience of being part of a crowd, of being unnoticed. I've always been at the mercy of people's judgments. "Am I accepted? Am I OK?" I could never just hang out and be a kid among kids or a young man among young men.

What I didn't know during those years of panic is that while, yes, my disorders made me the one in a billion kid, the truth is the same for me as it is for anyone else, anyone "normal": It's up to me to tolerate, accept, or even love myself and stop all of this worrying. It's not up to others to change their behavior or their judgment. It's up to me to accept myself.

Today, when I go around the country and give my speeches, when I go through my life, when I'm doing all the things that make me be me, I don't bother thinking or explaining to people, "Please!! Love me. I'm cool!" Instead, I recognize that others don't t know what's going on in my life, the same as I don't know what's going on in theirs. That's our starting point.

Not long ago, I went to an Amtrak station in Albany, New York. I was on my way to a speaking gig in Washington. I entered the station to find myself in a huge atrium with lots of windows. It was the kind of space where noises tend to echo – the kind of space where a guy with lots of loud verbal tics could cause alarm and attract unwanted attention.

Because my tics had abated, however, no one noticed me. I didn't alarm anyone. I didn't have to explain anything. I didn't have to feel stupid or embarrassed. For one of the first times in my life, I got to move through a crowd without attracting any undue attention. I was simply allowed to be there. To exist.

When my train came, I boarded and began looking for a seat. The first open seat I saw was next to a black man. There were other seats available. For a second, I considered sitting in one of them because I didn't want to freak the man out with my tics. But, for the first time in my life, I had the confidence that I could get through the experience without ticcing. I was having a good day. Why not push my luck?

I did it. I sat next to the guy. I didn't make any announcements. I didn't tell him I have TS. I didn't apologize to him for all the things I was inevitably going to say that would offend him. And then we rode. Three hours. I had a couple of teeth clenches and a couple of sniffs. But that was it. And the whole time, I was marveling, "This is what life is like? I can just do whatever I want and not have to apologize? Nobody cares about me!" It was exhilarating in a way that is hard to express unless you've ever been released from the weight of something enormous. Normal life becomes a miracle. And that's more and more how I feel these days. Every bit of progress is a miracle.

I chart these miracles one by one. Naturally, at least one of them has to do with pooping. It happened in November 2010. It was the moment I finally learned to fully tolerate the idea of someone close to me hearing me poop.

I have a friend named Jamie. She has horrible OCD. Although hers is very different from mine, we relate very well because of our shared struggles. Unlike me, she's great with relationships. She's had the same boyfriend for 10 years. She told me once that her boyfriend comes into the bathroom sometimes and kisses her while she's pooping. What hit me when she told me this was jealousy. I thought, "Wow, if I could ever have that, that would be the definition of love. That would do it for me. I'd finally know this person loves me."

You have to remember: This has been the single aspect of my life that has made me the most scared of other people. It's been the thing that has made me feel most separated from other people. I had never been able to grow out of being the traumatized little kid with diapers at the sleepover. This was something that still got in the way of all my relationships.

So, in November 2010, I was at my apartment in Boston. Four of us share the apartment, but we only have three bathrooms. You can see where this is going, I bet: I have to share a bathroom.

One night, my friend Ross was brushing his teeth in the bathroom we share, and I said, "You know what? My biggest fear has always been pooping in front of someone."

Without missing a beat, he said, "Dude, go for it. Go ahead. Do it right now." It was kind of like a dare.

I sat down on the toilet. And I have to tell you, weird as it sounds, it was an incredible moment. He finished brushing his teeth, and I was still on the toilet, doing my noisy thing. He didn't leave. He just stood there. Finally, I asked, "What are you doing?" He said, "I'm waiting for you to finish!" Because he knew it was my greatest fear!

I've made enormous progress learning how to Live and Let Live with my own behaviors. I still sniff on people all the time. It's one of my oldest tics. By and large, however, I've stopped worrying about it. It's just not the end of the world. Live and Let Live.

But pooping? It's still a big deal.

I was in the Atlanta airport not long ago. I went to the bathroom and, when I walked out, a custodian was shaking his head in disbelief. He said to me, "You are not a human being." I kind of chuckled,

looked back at him and said, "Sir, I don't have most of my intestines."
And he said, "I could tell."

On that same trip, I was at a restaurant, going to the bathroom, when I heard a kid say to his father, "Daddy, is that the diarrhea monster?" The diarrhea monster! -It was hilarious. I kind of wanted to grab the boy's ankle and make some scary noise – some *other* scary noise.

My attitude now is a far cry from the old days when I would be at a restaurant bathroom and, if someone came in, I'd stop whatever I was doing. I'd halt. Pause. And wait. If I made even a sound, I'd curdle with shame.

I know now that if I'm going to the bathroom in public and I'm worried about the person next to me, I'm being crazy. At the very most, all I know of them is the two inches of their shoe I can see from underneath the stall. I don't know if they hate me. I don't know if they're deaf and can't even hear me. I don't know anything about them. Until I do, there's no reason for me to make any assumptions about what they're thinking. I can keep my fears and discomfort in check.

Things are getting even better than that. Because I'm truly learning how not to care. How to Live and Let Live. How to just live my life and live up to my own message.

Last winter, some friends and I went to a bar in Boston called the Harp. It was freezing cold, and I was standing outside in line with my best friend, Andy. Two really cute women were waiting behind us in line. We made eye contact and were close enough to hear each other's conversations. Not long ago, I would have turned to them and said, "Yo, I just want to give you a heads up. I have Tourette syndrome."

But this time, I relaxed, said nothing and decided to try a little experiment.

As we stood there, I occasionally chomped my teeth and barked. They didn't say anything. I took a dose of my own medicine. I made a list. "Marc, what are all the things you're afraid of here? What might they be thinking about you? What's the worst thing that could happen?"

I went through my usual list. They would think I was weird. They would think I was gross. They'd hate me. By hating me, they would just be two more girls in a long, long line of girls who will all hate me. Forever. Until I die, alone, naked, homeless because, of course, no one will ever hire me for a job because I'm so disg—

No, I'm just kidding. It didn't go that far. I realized before I got that far, "OK, dude. You're insane."

I've been told this many times, and I understand it, but I never believed it: "If you only knew how little other people cared about you, you would be shocked." I have always believed this might be true for other people but never for me. But that night when I started going down my long, silly list of fears, I realized it had to be true. There's no way these women had the energy to think so much about me and all the things wrong with me. It was just me, alone, doing this to myself. I decided to try not doing it and see what happened.

We finally made our way into the club, and my friends and I began dancing. I had completely forgotten about those two women. All of a sudden, I bumped into one of them. To finish my little experiment, I asked her, "Listen, I know it's bizarre, but what were you thinking of me when I was doing all this stuff while we were in line?"

She looked surprised. "Why, what were you doing? What stuff?" She hadn't noticed anything unusual at all.

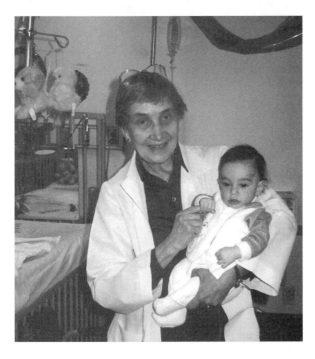

In the photo above, my mom and dad, Iris and Bill, and my big brother, Brian, are holding me at the hospital when I was just 7 days old. At left, Dr. Jesse Ternberg, the doctor who saved my life, called me her "tough bird" after I survived a severe intestinal birth defect.

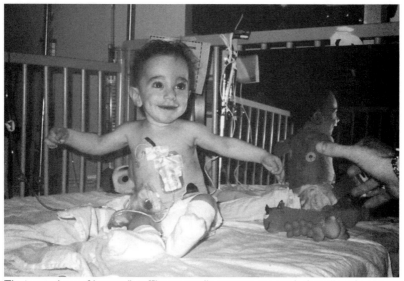

That sexy bag of brown "stuff" was my ileostomy, a pouch that directly connected to my intestines through my stomach.

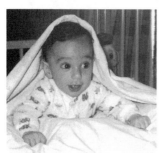

My family made my hospital bed a photography studio.

On my 2nd birthday, after another major surgery, Mickey came to try to cheer me up after illness abruptly ended our trip to Disney World.

No one would have guessed that by age 3 I had already undergone five major surgeries.

In middle school, I created a toy sale with the help of friends and donated all of the money to the playroom at the St. Louis Children's Hospital.

Clockwise from left: adventures at Boy Scout Camp; the moment I left the hospital once and for all at age 4, I began dreaming about becoming a doctor; in high school, I played soccer, tennis and even tried football junior year. Football was a mistake!

Nothing like family vacation photos! It's funny how Justin is now taller than I am.

Two of my best friends, my little brother Justin and my older brother Brian.

A St. Louis Post-Dispatch photographer is responsible for this best tic ever captured as a photo. The picture was taken during play rehearsal.

Dancing like no one is watching with one of my earliest friends from life, Jodie.

Cookie Monster, the Count, Oscar the Grouch, and Elmo, a.k.a some of my best friends from high school and roommates while living in Boston (Mike, Me, Ross & Greg).

Dr. Ternberg and I visited the St. Louis Zoo Penguin Exhibit right after I graduated high school.

A photographer from suburban Chicago's Daily Herald took this picture from my 10th speaking engagement during my year off before medical school. I spoke to 1,500 students at Carmel Catholic High School outside of Chicago.

About the Author

Two days after Marc Elliot was born, he was diagnosed with a rare birth defect called Hirschsprung's disease. Hirschsprung's had given him almost no working intestines and no ability to digest food on his own. Despite high odds of death or a horrible quality of life, one brave surgeon, Dr. Jesse Ternberg, took Marc under her wings, took a chance and saved his life. After spending the first six months of his life in St. Louis Children's Hospital, undergoing seven experimental surgeries, Marc became known as the "miracle baby."

However, Marc's challenges did not end after he left the hospital. At the age of nine, he was diagnosed with Tourette syndrome, a neurological disorder that causes him to make involuntary motor and vocal tics. As Marc grew older, his tics manifested in many different ways, from "ticcing" inappropriate words to blurting out random noises, including barking like a dog and chomping his teeth.

Over the next 10 years, Marc struggled to live a normal life in the suburbs of St. Louis. Aside from the scars that stretched across his abdomen and the frequent outbursts of tics and and offensive language, Marc lived with a special enthusiasm for life. He was a talented thespian, was active in tons of sports, and even was elected student body president of his high school.

Marc attended Washington University in St. Louis, where he majored in biology and pursued a pre-medicine path in hopes of following in the footsteps of the pediatric surgeon who saved his life. After graduating in May 2008, Marc embarked on a nationwide speaking tour. The tour was intended as "just something to do" before he became a doctor. His subject was tolerance.

In his presentation, "What Makes You Tic?" he drew on his experiences of not fitting in, of not feeling comfortable with others, to discuss fundamental lessons about tolerance — how to live with our own and others' differences. Little did he know this would become his calling.

Over the past three years, Marc has spoken to hundreds of groups and organizations, reaching out to more than 100,000 individuals in the United States and internationally. At the age of 26, Marc has now found a way to use his own story, his triumph over handicaps, as a way of helping individuals around the world find their own path to tolerance — for themselves and others.